MW00465369

Quantum Forgiveness: Physics, Meet Jesus
by David Hoffmeister
ISBN: 978-1-942253-16-7

Copyright © 2015
Living Miracles Publications

First Printed Edition 2015

Living Miracles Publications
P.O. Box 789, Kamas, UT 84036 USA
publishing@livingmiraclescenter.org
+1 435.200.4076

LIVING MIRACLES

This book was joyfully produced by the Living Miracles Community—a non-profit ministry run by inspired modern-day mystics devoted to awakening.

QUANTUM
FORGIVENESS
Physics, Meet Jesus

David Hoffmeister

DAVID HOFFMEISTER

Mystic David Hoffmeister is a living demonstration that peace is possible. His gentle demeanor and articulate, non-compromising expression are a gift to all. He is known for his practical application of the non-dual teachings necessary to experience the Unified Mind. His clarity about the function of forgiveness in spiritual awakening and his radical use of mindful movie-watching in the release of judgment is unsurpassed. The purity of the message he shares points directly to the Source. Over the past 29 years, David has traveled to 41 countries across 6 continents to extend the message that Truth is available for everyone, now.

David's message speaks to all people, regardless of whether their background is religious, spiritual, or scientific. He is as comfortable delving into the metaphysics of the movie *The Matrix,* as he is in pointing to the underlying meaning of the scriptures in the Bible.

David's own journey involved the study of many pathways, culminating in a deeply committed practical application of *A Course in Miracles,* of which he is a renowned teacher. His teachings have been translated into 13 languages, and taken into the hearts and minds of millions through the intimate style of his books, audios, and videos.

The mystical experience is one of clarity, great joy, deep peace, and tranquility—it ends the world of duality and conflict forever. The experience is not of this world, but radiates from within. It is not a concept; it comes into awareness when all concepts have been laid by.

FOREWORD

As a kid, one of my favorite TV producers was Gene Roddenberry, the creator of the often-brilliantly-insightful *Star Trek* television and film franchise. In my opinion, he didn't get it quite right when he started the shows and films off with the immortal words, "Space—the final frontier." It would be more accurate to say, "Headspace—the final frontier!" Mind, as non-dualists understand, is the Alpha and the Omega—where everything starts and it all ends.

David Hoffmeister's latest book, *Quantum Forgiveness: Physics, Meet Jesus*, reminds us that in watching movies we can gather insight into the alternate story the ego concocted—that time and space—is one, big, elaborate, illusory dream. One that in fact we had no idea that we were participating in. While only the truth is true, it seems that we need tools to undo this ego invention.

David has been teaching for years that we can use *film* as such a tool. Like the Indian sage Ramana Maharshi suggested, we can use a splinter to remove a splinter. *Quantum Forgiveness* shows us how to use the "splinter" of film to undo the "splinter" known as "the ego dream," as both "splinters" are illusory.

Deep down, what do we all want? We want peace of mind, above all else. We want to turn off the incessant "hypothetical generator" in our heads, the internal "Holodeck" where we constantly grieve about the past and fret about the future.

David uses the tool of film in this book to remind us that the path of peace and salvation need not be one of pain. In fact, we can use entertainment as a means to undo guilt. After all, as *A Course in Miracles* says, "Into eternity, where all is one, there crept a tiny, mad idea, at which the Son of God remembered not to laugh." Instead of self-flagellation, the Course strongly suggests we take a light-hearted approach to salvation, joyfully laughing along the way, and what better way than through the illustrative medium of film, which lends itself to many profound 'ah-ha' moments!

Page after page, *Quantum Forgiveness* offers the reader an experience, a spectacular way of coming to "Know Thyself" by using guided movie-watching that is specifically tailored for awakening.

This book's subtitle: "Physics, Meet Jesus," foreshadows a major theme in this latest work. David reminds us that the Course counsels us to have the determination to question everything, much like quantum physicists questioned everything about Newtonian physics. In so doing, what passed as "common knowledge" can be exposed as false, like Toto pulling back the curtain to reveal the truth about the Wizard of Oz. I have found this book to be a well written, entertaining, and an enlightened approach to do just that!

In short, *Quantum Forgiveness: Physics, Meet Jesus* is a thrilling, fantastic deep-dive on how to use film to facilitate the celestial speed-up.

Robert Capozzi
Author
Reel Vision: Unlocking Metaphysical Meaning in Movies, Volume 1
Bellport, NY

EDITOR'S NOTE

The content in this book consists of lightly edited transcripts of talks given by David Hoffmeister during various movie gatherings.

BIBLIOGRAPHY

A Course in Miracles
Second edition, 1996

Foundation for Inner Peace
P.O. Box 598
Mill Valley, CA 94942
www.acim.org

Course quotes are referenced using the following system:
T: Text
W: Workbook for Students
M: Manual for Teachers

Example:
"All real pleasure comes from doing God's Will." T-1.VII.1
T-1.VII.1 = Text, Chapter 1, Section VII, paragraph 1

Quotes originating from the Workbook Lessons are referenced without the paragraph number.
Example: W-132

TIPS ON HOW TO USE THIS BOOK

You need not enjoy movie-watching to receive the profound gift of this book. The text is a complete teaching in and of itself, offering a portal of awakening for any open mind. However, if you would like to watch the movie as part of the healing experience, we recommend the following steps.

Step One:

Read the corresponding chapter before you watch the movie. This will help you prepare your mind to see the symbols and characters of the movie as "pointers" to the truth. The chapters provide a discussion that goes deeply into the lessons of the movie, offering clarity and solidifying the healing benefits in the mind.

Step Two:

Watch the movie. Be willing to stop the movie in order to detach from intense scenes, attractive scenarios, or moments when you want to know what will happen next. Watch your emotions and the investment you have in the images. Even if you experience discomfort, try not to distract away from it. Give yourself permission to stop investigating and just be with what is arising in awareness.

Step Three:

Reread the chapter and rewatch the movie until you feel you have moved from an intellectual understanding to an actual experience of the Truth. Ask Spirit to guide the direction of your thinking while you are reading and watching.

Enjoy waking up with the movies!

Why wait for the drama to play out in your life, when you can let the character on the screen do it for you?

TABLE OF CONTENTS

Chapter 1

AWAKENING WITH THE MOVIES

Jesus shared his profound wisdom, light, and love through the use of parables. He taught from a fishing boat, from the mount, during meals, or anywhere he was amongst people. He was a public mystic; his was a ministry that demonstrated the Christ. Jesus used parables because he wanted people to be able to relate to his teachings.

That is what I do in my travels and journeys; movies are modern-day parables. I use them as teaching demonstrations because people can relate to them; while watching a movie they can relax and let their hearts open up. Watching movies is an enjoyable way to wake up and heal. It is not as threatening as being, for example, in a family situation or confrontational relationship. Movies can help to "collapse time" in the sense that they can be used to get in touch with the unconscious in an experiential way.

Spirit showed me techniques for watching movies in a new way—not as entertainment or escapism, but as a way in which people could allow intense emotions to arise for healing. When I hold movie gatherings, I don't show movies straight through because they can trigger memories and emotions that have been repressed and denied. I pause the film when people have these intense emotions come up so that we can be present with whatever is arising for healing in the moment. It's important to realize that the subconscious has to come up. We welcome the feelings so that they can be released for healing, and a new perspective can come in. When invited, Spirit provides a safe presence for the subconscious to arise without any judgment. It is beautiful to join with people in this heart-to-heart way. That is one of my big messages. Movies can open the mind to a more expansive awareness of our True Nature and Identity.

Sharing movies with others over the years has been amazing. Spirit comes through me with movie set-ups and commentary about the deeper messages and the symbols within the films that really "hit home." I have gotten wonderful feedback and responses. I remember an elderly couple who had never seen *The Matrix*. Based on the movie trailers they were not sure they wanted to see it. But they came to one of my movie gatherings and I gave a thorough set-up of the metaphysics and the context, and explained how helpful watching this movie could be. As we watched the movie, I paused frequently and gave inspired commentary. At the end they said, "We are so glad we watched it with you because you were a guide for us." They had big smiles on their faces and felt fulfilled.

When I show a relationship movie like *Eternal Sunshine of the Spotless Mind*, the young couples in the audience have sparkly eyes after the discussion at the end of the movie. They seem to be seeing some of the blocks in their consciousness, in their relationships, for the first time. They are filled with gratitude for this inroad into the unconscious that brings the darkness up and out, and does it in a way that they find enjoyable.

In the last few years, many absolutely spectacular quantum movies have been made. I call them quantum movies because they can't be followed in the old movie-watching ways. If we are looking for a plot or a storyline, that's not going to work because these movies are way past that! It takes a lot of inspiration and interpretation to draw meaning from them because although the meaning is within us, it is covered over by familiar linear constructs. We must step back in our mind and allow the experience. We must invite Spirit into our mind as we watch and ask to be shown, "What is the lesson here?"

When we are willing to be shown, the lesson can be revealed. Quantum movies are helpful because they provide a broader spectrum and perspective than we are used to. The Workbook Lessons in *A Course in Miracles* are part of a system designed to give us an experience. Quantum movies can do the same thing. The Holy Spirit can use both in a very direct way to help us spring into a place of not understanding what anything is for.

In this book, I have selected seven quantum movies that carry direct healing messages. These movies are powerful because they clearly depict the truth of Jesus' spiritual teachings from *A Course in Miracles*; they contain the same deep wisdom, light, and love that Jesus demonstrated. Quantum movies propel us into a direct experience that is aligned with the world-changing perspective of quantum physics. The profound lessons from these movies are directly relevant to the core concerns of life; they are helping us to see all of the ego's myriad tricks—the belief in history, ambitions, goals, outcomes, and so forth. The Holy Spirit is now using Hollywood to reach the sleeping mind! Holy Spirit has infiltrated Hollywood!

This book is our prayer to Spirit: Make everything new! Show us the world anew—fresh, clean, and clear! Then we have nothing to worry about. When we trust, listen to, and follow Spirit, it is game over for the ego. Game over for worry, sadness, and anxiety. As Jesus says in the Course, "Trust would settle every problem now!" Happiness is Who We Are Now!

Chapter 2

WHAT IS QUANTUM FORGIVENESS?

Quantum physics experiments have demonstrated that the expectations of the observer determine the result of the experiment. In other words, there is no split between the observer and the observed, the subject and the object. The world we're looking upon is entirely subjective; there is not an objective world apart from our mind. We are simply observing what we believe being acted out in form. No two people share the same world because the world is completely subjective. Jesus states, "There is no world apart from what you wish. There is no world!" W-132 He also says, "I have given everything I see all the meaning it has for me." W-2

For centuries, science has operated on the premise that there is an external world that is observable and measurable, and that the experimenter is separate from that empirical world. The major discovery of quantum physics, several decades ago, was that there is not an external world outside of consciousness. I was quite excited about this discovery, which supports the interpretation that there is no world outside the mind of the perceiver. Everything is completely unified, completely connected; there is no separation. Everything is energy.

I have always been interested in working with *A Course in Miracles* and with the ideas of quantum physics. When we talk about going into the quantum field or about true forgiveness, which is that beautiful state of non-judgment, we are talking about the same thing. Mystics and saints, and now quantum physicists, are talking about the same experience, and so it seems quite natural for me to put those terms together: Quantum Forgiveness.

This is the same experience Jesus points to in *A Course in Miracles* when he talks about unified perception. He also calls it "the happy dream" or "true perception." I am amazed at how many roads there are that point to this same experience, and it is my joy and happiness to share this message.

I was raised in Christianity, which has an association with wrong-doing, with some sense of wrongness. But I've found that when we open up and start to come into an experience of deep peace and innocence—even when it's just a glimpse—we get a strong awareness of never having done anything wrong. Our perception shifts in a way that allows us to see peace. We do not have to work it out—it is like a state of grace. That grace has always been our nature; all we need to do is accept it. Once we do, we see that there never was a problem. God created us perfect; we have always been perfect in our Source. We want to go beyond the perspective of believing that there is a God out there somewhere. We want to see that our home is in our heart and that we have never left it.

In his movie *The Horse Whisperer*, Robert Redford helps a traumatized girl go through a healing experience with her horse. I saw a documentary about the man who was the consultant for that movie. His name was Buck, and he had transcended a traumatic childhood; he chose not to see himself as a victim. He showed his integrity, calmness, gentleness, and compassion in day-to-day living with people and horses. Buck has the ability to ride a horse almost as if he were in the quantum field. The horse flows so beautifully as an extension of his love. Buck is a beautiful witness of deep humility and simplicity. I love movies that show grace in motion, where the innocence is tangible. I am so grateful that we, like Buck, can choose the miracle.

I like to think of miracles as being very natural. I call them ordinary miracles. We do not need to be given extreme signs and symbols. We just need to experience the comforting, peaceful, still awareness that is always in us. It is Who we are. I like the idea that we are the living representations of love and light and joy. That is the burning fire in my heart. That is why I have traveled around the world so extensively, and why I am so comfortable being with my brothers and sisters wherever I go, regardless of what they profess to believe or not believe. I feel a deep connection to them that seems so natural. It is our Purpose to be in that experience and extend it. That is what I feel our lives are meant for. My life has been fully used to extend the Presence of Love.

True Love wants to come through in ways that people can relate to. People are not really interested in a lot of theory and theology; they want the experience. They want signs and symbols that are as simple as shaking hands, or hugging, or embracing, or just softly gazing into another's eyes. Although these gentle expressions come through what seems to be our human nature, it is really our divinity shining out.

Quantum physics shows us that everything we perceive is really just our state of mind. The body, with which we closely identify, acts as a barometer. It mirrors our state of mind in a very direct way. Whenever there seems to be discomfort or disease, we can see that as a gift which is signaling that we are having discomforting thoughts. We can go within, release those thoughts, and discover that we have no real reason to be ill. We are innocent; our natural inheritance is happiness, peace, and joy. So we can thank the body for being such a clear witness to our state of mind. In a biofeedback sense, it is helpful in coming to a state of True Quantum Forgiveness because we can be very honest with ourselves about how we feel. We do not have to stick with the idea that there is some external cause. We can start to take full responsibility for our state of mind.

Many movies have been made that also remind the mind that it made it all up: *The Truman Show, Groundhog Day, Dark City, Lucy,* and *Solaris.* Often, after watching one of these spectacular metaphysical movies, someone will ask, "Who wrote the movie, were they into the Course? Were the Wachowski brothers, who wrote and directed *The Matrix,* into the Course?" Actually, they were not. But they used a lot of great metaphysics to put it together. There are no writers out there, no directors, producers, or actors. Quantum movies are a symbolic representation of our mind's desire to wake up. We can think of them as catalysts for a quantum shift in mind.

The early scientists who discovered the atom, with its protons, neutrons, and electrons, believed they had discovered a solid thing. The body seems solid and the world seems solid, but quantum physics has shown us that there are no solid particles. Particles are just potentials and the world is merely thoughts and beliefs. We're dealing with a world of ideas. We may think that we have thoughts and that the thoughts can be manifested, but even manifesting is part of duality. There is no difference between thoughts and "manifested" thoughts.

What I found helpful with the Workbook Lessons of *A Course in Miracles* in regards to quantum physics is that the Course bridges the gap. It teaches that the thoughts we think we think and the world we think we see are the same. The beliefs that we hold and the world that we believe is external to the mind are actually the same. So we are literally doing everything to ourselves. The good news is that when we forgive, we are not forgiving something that seems to have been done to us—we are forgiving something that never happened. The separation is a hallucination. It is not a reality; it is not the Truth. It's an amazing Quantum Forgiveness moment when we have that realization.

I am very excited about Quantum Forgiveness. The pioneers of quantum physics overturned and transcended Newtonian physics and the scientific method. Quantum physicists worked down to the smallest units and realized that everything they thought they knew about the world was not true. The world is about potentiality. In superposition, for example, things appear where we believe they will appear. And that is exciting because it is a scientific discovery that does not have to stay in the lab. It actually has everything to do with who we are. It is the gateway to our experience of being one with Source!

We are on the threshold of this experience. There is a scene in the movie *Solaris* where one of the characters has been having fearful separation thoughts, and his partner says to him, "We don't have to think like that anymore." We are moving away from stories, linear perceptions, and grievances to a whole new way of thinking, in which we are whole and complete and innocent. It is truly thrilling to know that we are on the cusp of that right now. It is not something that we have to wait for. The Truth is right here, right now, patiently saying, "Here I am." Awakening is indeed a glorious journey of miracles and discoveries, and I feel so honored to be a full participant in it.

Chapter 3

MR. NOBODY

A World of Hypotheticals

As a child and teenager, I loved sports. Growing up, I would sit in front of the TV and, no matter what sport I was watching, I would work up a good sweat, as I was rooting for one side or the other. I was vocal about bad referee or umpire calls and I would yell at the television, "Oh! Terrible call! They would have scored if you hadn't made that call!"

My grandfather, Heinrich Herman Hoffmeister, would sit there with a twinkle in his eye and a big smile on his face as I gyrated all over the place. He would laugh and laugh at my many "if" statements: If the center fielder hadn't missed that ball, we would have shut them out! If the ref had made the right call we would've won. When the game was over, he would raise his finger and say, with a big smile, "If. It's the largest word in the English language!" Although I didn't realize it at the time, my grandfather was my first *A Course in Miracles* teacher. Using my love of sports, he was teaching me about hypotheticals.

Merriam-Webster defines a hypothetical as "not real: imagined as an example." Urban dictionary describes it as "something that exists as a possibility." My grandfather was saying it was a waste of time to worry or get upset about things that "could" or "should" have happened; that is, to react to a result that existed only in my imagination! That made sense to me, but eventually I started to think in even deeper terms. When I began studying the Course, I realized that the world of form is based on the premise that we could separate from God. Since that premise is false, that means the entire world is just a projection of the ego mind. Everything we see is nothing more than made-up, illusory images. The entire cosmos is the result of the belief that we are separate from God.

That means everything in the cosmos is a hypothetical! Everything is only "imagined as an example."

How is this possible? What does it look like? What does it mean in terms of awakening? The Course gives us quite a clue with the line, "History would not exist if you did not keep making the same mistake in the present." T-4.II-1.3 What a statement! It's an exciting invitation to look more deeply at the world we think we know.

It takes enormous willingness to consider the idea that everything in time and space is hypothetical. It takes going down the rabbit hole and then some. But the gift that awaits us as we start to align with the Truth is more fulfilling than anything we can imagine. *Mr. Nobody* takes us on a journey that beautifully dismantles the world of form, of cause and effect, and shows what happens when we let go of our desire to stay distracted by a made-up world.

Key Themes

- Hypothetical Choice
- Cause-and-Effect Relationships
- Linear versus Simultaneous Time

Movie Synopsis

Mr. Nobody is a tale about choice. Nemo, a nine-year-old boy, has been thrust into a position where he must make an impossible decision—to choose between his mother and father. In the seconds preceding the rest of his life he wonders where each choice will take him. 109 years later, Nemo is recounting his life story to a reporter. He seems to be very confused. He recounts his life from three primary points: at age nine when his parents divorced, at age fifteen when he fell in love, and at age thirty-four as an adult. All three unfold into their many possible outcomes. Were any of his lives real or were they all a figment of his imagination?

Introduction

The movie *Mr. Nobody* examines the core belief that we can find happiness if we make the right choices in life. We can't; it's impossible. But the belief that we have real choices that can bring us what we want is cherished by the ego because it keeps us locked into a never-ending quest of looking for happiness where it can't be found. *Mr. Nobody* demonstrates that all the choices of this world are made because we have forgotten God and therefore believe in an illusory world of duality. None of our choices are real because they are a choice between the images of this made-up world; that is, a choice between illusions. They are nothing more than hypotheticals, which serve as meaningless distractions.

In the movie, Nemo Nobody is the world's oldest mortal, who tells his story through flashbacks of what he remembers about his life. Nemo's experiences seem to involve several life scripts. For example, as a boy, Nemo has to choose whether to live with his father or his mother. The film shows each of these choices playing out over multiple lifetime scenarios with multiple life partners, and none of them work out happily. However, this is good news! The realization that nothing we've tried will ever work and that choices in form are meaningless is cause for celebration. Choices can exist only in duality, not in Oneness. But the sleeping mind has forgotten its Oneness; it has forgotten Heaven. It exists in a realm where there seem to be numerous choices, but really they are pseudo-choices. They are little snippets that reflect our fragmented desires and wishes.

Our certainty that we can make real choices is based on our belief in cause-and-effect relationships. Newtonian physics teaches that cause and effect are split—that cause comes first and effect comes second. It states that for every action, there is a reaction. The Course, however, teaches us that cause and effect are simultaneous. When we start to really understand this, we can see that everything we have believed in this world has no validity or reality; we can see that everything we have been taught is false. The seeming effects of the world all come from a false cause—the belief that we have separated from our Source. But ideas cannot leave their source; therefore, cause and effect cannot be separate.

In the Course, Jesus states, "The ego's teaching produces immediate results, because its decisions are immediately accepted as your choice. And this acceptance means that you are willing to judge yourself accordingly. Cause and effect are very clear in the ego's thought system, because all your learning has been directed toward establishing the relationship between them. And would you not have faith in what you have so diligently taught yourself to believe? Yet remember how much care you have exerted in choosing its witnesses, and in avoiding those which spoke for the cause of truth and its effects." T-16.III.2

The entire world of form is based on the false belief that cause and effect are separate; linear time itself is sustained only by the ego's insistence that there is causation in the world. We have learned this world carefully, and given credence to its upside down and backward thinking, where cause and effect have been reversed. The ego has put enormous effort in presenting it that way in order that we will not see the Truth. For example, when we experience traumatic events in our lives, we believe that those events cause a lasting effect on the mind. We don't see that the mind already believes it is guilty and is simply calling forth witnesses—in the form of painful or frightening experiences—to reinforce that guilt. Through the ego's lens, these events are viewed as causative instead of as reflections of the guilt and fear that are already present.

Mr. Nobody exposes the falsity of these beliefs. By using many examples of seeming cause-and-effect situations that are impossible to make sense of, it helps us unplug from the mentality that there is any causation whatsoever in form. The dismantling of cause-and-effect relationships is extremely disorienting to the ego mind, which demands to know, "What is going on here?" *Mr. Nobody* answers this question beautifully: There is nothing going on here. We can't figure out or understand the world. To see this with the Spirit's help is a great leap forward in consciousness.

Mr. Nobody contains a lot of scenes and information that the mind will want to try and organize in terms of linear time. The movie makes this quite difficult! For example, during the film, Nemo seems to age from a pre-natal state to 118 years old. But the scenes of his life are cut and spliced in a way that undoes the linear perspective. The two different scenarios that seem to result from Nemo's choice to live with his mom and then his choice to live with his dad play out back and forth. The scenes of Nemo's relationship with three different women are shuffled in a confusing manner. These montages are masterfully put together in a way that helps the ego mind start to loosen from the belief in time and space. They beautifully illustrate the ego's manipulation of images in the sleeping mind and how linear time is just a construct that covers over simultaneity.

The deepest teachings of *A Course in Miracles* are about the belief in linear time. The ego made linear time so that we could avoid aligning our mind with the Holy Spirit; that is, accepting the Atonement. The Atonement is the Holy Spirit's plan of correction for undoing the ego and healing the belief in separation; its principle is that the separation never occurred.

The ego, however, will do anything to convince us that the separation is real because once we accept the Atonement the ego is out of business. A good question to ask in any situation is: Will this reinforce or loosen my belief in linear time? *A Course in Miracles* teaches that time is transcended in the holy instant, which is an instant in which we choose the Holy Spirit instead of the ego. As we undo the belief in linear time, and our attachment to specifics, we rise to the dreamer-of-the-dream perspective. This is the only experience that can bring us true freedom and happiness.

David's Movie Commentary

Scene: The introductory scene shows a pigeon in a training box. A voice-over explains what is happening: Like most living creatures, the pigeon quickly associates the pressing of the lever with a reward. But when a timer releases the seed automatically every twenty seconds, the pigeon wonders, "What did I do to deserve this?" If it was flapping its wings at the time, it will continue to flap, convinced that its actions have a decisive influence on what happens.

This scene demonstrates learned behavior. Because the pigeon flapped its wings at the exact same time the random treat was given, it made the association that its wing-flapping caused the treat to appear. He then repeats the behavior over and over in order to elicit the same response. This scene perfectly sets up the movie because the pigeon, like all of us, has been taught to believe in cause and effect. We think that something we have done produces a reaction. We wonder, "What action did I take in form to make this happen? That is, what did I do to deserve this?"

Scene: *Nemo is shown as a dead body, then as drowning in his car, then as being shot.*

The first scene shows Nemo as a dead body in a morgue. Immediately after that, he is seen underwater in a car, and then being shot in a bathtub. Nemo, in a voice-over, asks, "What did I do to deserve this?"

The ego immediately begins looking for what precipitated Nemo's death, just like it does when it watches a news program about a murder. That's because the ego always has a need to know what happened; in fact, the world revolves around the attempt to find causation in form. For example, if someone has symptoms of an illness, they go to a doctor to get a diagnosis and find a solution. If someone is abandoned by their partner, they are likely to go over and over the relationship in their mind, trying to figure out what happened. If a plane crashes, investigators spend months or even years trying to determine why it went down.

The ego's entire purpose for time and space is to look for cause-and-effect answers in a linear, or form-based, way. That's what all the questions of the world are about. Even when we get into spiritual awakening, there are still many questions regarding form. Practical questions such as, "What step do I need to take next?" may also arise. However, even this question indicates that we are looking for direction in form. If we asked Jesus what our next step is, He would tell us that it is the holy instant. But if our mind can't comprehend what that means, then we're not ready for it. Therefore, the Spirit has to come into our conscious awareness through the use of symbols.

Scene: *Nemo, as an old man, is meeting with a psychotherapist. He has no idea who he is or where he is located in time or space. He seems to be remembering simultaneous life scenarios.*

The psychotherapist, like the ego, asks form-related questions. When he asks Nemo how old he is, Nemo states that he is thirty-four. The therapist asks him to look at his hands and then in the mirror, because Nemo's answer and the physical evidence do not match up. Nemo is horrified and confused when he looks in the mirror and sees an old man. When the therapist tells him that he is 117, Nemo declares emphatically, "I've got to wake up. I've got to wake up!"

This desperation to understand who we are and what is happening lies beneath the ego's constant attempt to figure things out. It is what underlies the scientific attempt to figure out the building blocks of how the universe works. It is behind every question asked in inter-personal relationships. The ego tries frantically to make sense of everything it perceives because it is quite insecure. Its self-concept is very shaky. This movie illustrates that the reason for our desperation doesn't have anything to do with what's happening in the world of form—it comes from our belief in cause and effect. This false belief must be undone in order for us to experience the peace and stillness that is our natural inheritance.

Scene: A television host is doing a live show about Nemo. It is called "The Last Mortals." The host announces that Nemo will be the last man on earth to die of old age.

This scene shows a futuristic scenario involving the media. We learn that people no longer die because they are now able to get stem cells from pigs. We also discover that Nemo Nobody is the last living mortal. Nemo, who is in the hospital and has no idea who he is, allows the psychotherapist to try an "old" technique—hypnotiza-tion—to try and restore his memories.

Scene: Nemo remembers a pre-birth state in which Angels of Oblivion are erasing children's memories by touching their upper lips, leaving a mark. They forget to touch Nemo.

This scene demonstrates that before birth, everything is known. German philosopher Immanuel Kant spoke of this as a priori knowledge, meaning that we know all of the answers intuitively, independently of all particular experiences. However, if everything is forgotten after we are born because we have been touched by the Angels of Oblivion, our Source—God—is also forgotten.

In the world of form, the ego is the agent of oblivion. In fact, it made the world specifically as a hiding place where we could forget the Truth of who we are. We think that we have choices in this made-up world, and many people think that's exciting, but only meaningless choices are offered, choices without causes. Shakespeare described this as "Much ado about nothing." In the Course, Jesus says that all the roadways of the world "lead to death." T-31.IV.2 False choices are what sustain our belief in the world.

The Course points us in a different direction. It tells us to ask, in every situation, "What is it for? What is the purpose?" We can't find the answers in the world. Like Nemo, we've got to wake up.

Scene: *Nemo, as an adult, is giving a lecture on time.*

Nemo says, "What was there before the big bang? There *was* no before, because before the big bang, time did not exist. Time is a result of the expansion of the universe itself but what will happen when the universe has finished expanding and the movement is reversed? How do we distinguish between illusion and reality?"

This movie raises the quantum physics idea that time can run backwards as easily as forwards. This may be a helpful stepping stone for the mind, but In Oneness there is no time or space. Practically speaking, time and space lasted but a seeming instant and was simultaneously corrected by the Holy Spirit. Only because of the ego does this unreal instant seem to be repeated over and over and over again. The well-known Course phrase "the script is written" emphasizes that the dream of the world ended long ago. Time, practically speaking, is over and gone and in Reality never happened.

There are no choices in Heaven; there is nothing to choose among in Oneness. So the whole idea of choice between illusions in form must rest on the concept of linear time as opposed to simultaneous time.

The scene flashes back to Nemo as a child, looking at his dinner. He says, "If you mix the mashed potatoes and the sauce, you can't separate them later; it's forever." He looks at his father smoking and says, "The smoke comes out of Daddy's cigarette but it never goes back in. You cannot go back." This is followed by another flashback where the child Nemo is standing in front of a dessert buffet. In a voiceover, he says, "That's why it's hard to choose; you have to make the right choice. As long as you don't choose, everything remains possible."

Nemo is talking here about the importance of making the right choice. But by what basis do we determine what a right choice is? We try to make choices that better our life or our health or our financial situation—the list goes on and on. But what if it's all a farce that keeps us in an endless loop of choosing between things that aren't real? Since the dream of the world is over, that means that when we're trying to make a choice in form, we're trying to choose between the past and the past. Even though we think we're choosing something new, something different, something better, we're always choosing the past. How does that make anything better? That's the whole conundrum.

Scene: Nemo sees three young girls—Anna, Elise, and Jean—sitting on a bench.

These three girls are Nemo's future wives, but not due to polygamy! The three women that Nemo ends up marrying are each from a separate life scenario that is playing out simultaneously with the others. There's something about each woman that he's attracted to, but there's also a much deeper issue playing out. Nemo feels a sense of incompleteness, and he's trying to solve it in form. Each of the relationships seems to be the result of a choice, or decision, that Nemo has made, and they play out in form as scenarios. But they are all just thoughts. They are all just memories in the mind, based on preferences and the attempt to find love in form.

Nemo falls in love with Anna when they are children. As teenagers, they have an intense love affair but are parted by circumstance. Nemo searches for Anna throughout the movie but when he finally finds her, he loses her phone number and they are separated once more.

Nemo meets Elise at a high school dance where she is devastated because the object of her affections—Stefano—doesn't love her. Nemo plays the role of rescuer in the life scenario with Elise. They have three children, who she can't care for properly due to her deep depression. She spends much of her time in bed, crying. In another version of this life scenario, however, Elise is killed on their wedding day when a propane truck directly ahead of them in traffic explodes.

Prior to arriving at the same dance where he met Elise, Nemo decides to marry the first girl who dances with him, who happens to be Jean. Nemo didn't love her; he just turned to her when he couldn't have Elise. Nemo and Jean have the seeming perfect life: Lots of money, a big house with a pool, and two children. These three relationship scenarios wind throughout the movie in a manner that seems random, contradictory, and even impossible.

However, the movie shows all of the relationship patterns from a much larger perspective. We start to see that all of the fluctuating images in Nemo's life scenarios are distractions that keep his mind focused on the little picture. Eventually, the memory fragments will help him to see a much bigger picture, one far beyond conflict, choices, and constant compromise.

Scene: *Nemo, as a child, says, "Daddy says you can predict exactly when Mars will be in the sky, even in a hundred years, but the funny thing is, Daddy doesn't know what will happen to him two minutes from now."*

Nemo sees a vision of an accident that is about to happen. He runs out of the house to warn his dad, but it is too late. His dad, who has a piece of eggshell stuck in his mouth, is standing by the car, unaware that he has forgotten to put the hand-brake on. The car rolls down a hill and hits a mother and baby, killing them. Nemo's dad is traumatized.

The father seeming to cause someone's death seems like a cause-and-effect sequence. But really it is an interpretation that somebody caused something bad and now there are effects that are negative and very hard to deal with. *Mr. Nobody* breaks down what Jesus calls these spurious cause-effect relationships, which don't have any meaning in

Truth, by showing that they are all hypotheticals. None of the scenarios can be any different than they are. They are all exactly as they were called for from the mind, which is an impossible situation of duality and multiplicity.

The mind has been mesmerized into believing that there are causes and effects in the world, and there are almost endless examples that seem to back up this belief. If we don't pay the electric bill, the lights get turned off. If we don't put food into the body, it seems to get hungry. If we don't put food into the body for a prolonged period of time, like Gandhi, the body seems to get skinny. But every example is based on the *belief* in cause and effect. They are all just thoughts in the mind. We don't realize that everything that seems to be happening is all coming from consciousness and that, furthermore, it's not even real. What we see are meaningless bits of images and colors and shapes and sounds, cobbled together in a way that seems meaningful but isn't.

This movie questions cause-and-effect relationships and the choices we believe are so important. We spend so much time and effort trying to learn things and analyze things and figure things out, but we have no idea what is really happening.

Scene: Young Nemo sees Anna, one of his futures wives, at the swimming pool. A love song plays in the background.

This life scenario is the "soul mate" hypothetical. Everything was forgotten when we came into the world of form. But the mind knows on some level that something is missing. That something is Love; that something is God. Since we can't push love completely out of awareness, everyone who seems to come to this world will seek for it. However, love can never be found in external form. When Nemo sees Anna at the pool, it is the stuff of romance. He sees his "soul mate" for the first time—it's love at first sight. What Nemo is trying to find in this love partner, however, is what he believes he lacks within himself.

All of us are taught that we must seek outside of ourselves for completion. The ego wants us to think that what we are looking for—our "soul mate" or some other "missing piece"—is out in the world. But the ego's mantra is "seek and do not find," and it is this that keeps us in an endless, futile search. The only way out is to identify and release the mistaken belief in our mind that happiness can be found in an external source.

Scene: Young Nemo is on the train platform, holding both his mother's and his father's hands. The name of the train station is "Chance." His mother asks him, "So, Nemo, have you made up your mind? Do you want to come with me or do you want to stay with your father?" The train arrives, and his mother gets on and looks longingly at Nemo. He starts to run after the train while his father calls his name. He catches up and his mother pulls him onto the train. But the scene immediately replays and the second time, Nemo is unable to catch up with the train so he stays with his dad.

This is the pivotal scene in the film. Nemo seems to have a choice in the world of form—to stay with mom or to stay with dad. That's an interesting quandary because in Heaven we simply have one Parent, our Creator. The belief that we come from two should be a major clue that something strange is going on. We are a creation of a single Source, not two. In Heaven, there is only pure Oneness—and there are no choices to be made in pure Oneness. However, everything in the world of duality is the product of two, of opposites. And trying to make choices between imaginary images and imaginary options causes frustration, anxiety, and desperation. We want to make the right choice, but there is no right choice in form.

How can we "choose between" for love; how could that even be possible? It is an insane choice. And that's what is underneath this dualistic world where all meaning is projected out onto the images of absolutely impossible choices in form. Love doesn't choose. Love simply is. The mind when it's asleep, however, believes it has to choose.

Nemo loves both his mom and dad; the choice he is asked to make is impossible. Nemo believes that either option will result in pain, and throughout the movie, the seeming results of him choosing his mom and him choosing his dad play out. Within each seeming choice, other multiple scenarios play out as well. The realization we have to come to is that because every scenario is a thought in the mind, everything is happening simultaneously. There has to be a way out of this predicament, out of this strange, illusory world. Eventually, *Mr. Nobody* is going to show us what it is.

Scene: A teen-aged Nemo is sitting on the beach, watching people play in the water. Anna comes over and sits next to him, and invites him to swim with she and her friends. Nemo replies: "I don't go swimming with idiots."

With that one quick line, the soul mate scenario seems to go up in a puff of smoke! Anna responds, "You're a jerk" and leaves Nemo sitting by himself on the beach. When Nemo runs into Anna later in life, she is with her children. When the same beach scenario replays, however, it seems to have a different outcome. This time, when Anna invites Nemo to swim he says, "I don't know how to swim." Because Anna is attracted to Nemo's openness, she says, "I'll keep you company." Then they are shown as teenagers, having a sexual relationship.

Although cause and effect seems to be in play in each scenario, it isn't; all of the life scenarios in the movie are happening simultaneously. They only seem to play out as cause and effect because we believe in a world of causation. The mind, even while sleeping, is powerful—it is able to generate entire scenarios, entire lifetimes, with a single, errant thought. *However, none of what it generates is real; it is all just images of hypothetical situations.* That is why things can never make sense from a linear perspective, and why it is pointless to try and follow the threads of seeming cause-effect relationships.

Linear time is nothing more than the ego's attempt to hold cause and effect apart from each other. The Course teaches us that linear time is impossible because ideas leave not their source. Another way of saying this is that the mind gets exactly what it wants. And when it wants only peace it cannot perceive anything but a peaceful world. But as long as it is not sure about what it wants then there seems to be a gap between cause and effect. Even when Nemo seems to get everything he wants, he still is not happy; he still continues to play out hypotheticals in an attempt to find fulfillment in form.

Scene: *Nemo has been rejected by Elise and so he dances with Jean. As they ride home on his motorbike, Nemo's voice as a young child narrates. He says, "On that day, I will make a lot of foolish decisions."*

Nemo decides six things when he's riding home from the dance on his motorbike with Jean: "I will never leave anything to chance again. I will marry the girl on my motorbike. I'll be rich. We'll have a house, a big house, painted yellow, with a garden, and two children, Paul and Michael. I'll have a convertible, a red convertible, and a swimming pool. I'll learn to swim. I will not stop until I've succeeded."

There it is—the ego's insane thought system in a nutshell: "I won't stop until I succeed." We are convinced that we could be happy if only we could find the perfect circumstances in form. When we seem to get what we want, however, we quickly find that it doesn't bring lasting happiness. So we look again. And again and again and again. We keep making up hypothetical scenario after hypothetical scenario, lifetime after lifetime, in the hope that one of them will finally do the trick. As long as we have the belief "I am not as God created me," we will try to prove this over and over and over again. We will try everything we can think of, over as many millions of years as we want to take. And people think choice is a good thing! Choice is nothing but the big trick of this world. As long as we are choosing in form, we are choosing to be little time-bound creatures who are locked into birth and death, who will grow sick and suffer and die.

It can be helpful to think of all of the choices we make—who to meet, where to go, what to eat, what to do for a living—during the course of our life as an "idol package."

Jesus says in the Course, "What is an idol? Do you think you know? An idol is a wish, made tangible and given form, and thus perceived as real, and seen outside the mind. Yet it is still a thought, and cannot leave the mind that is its source. What purpose has an idol then? What is it for? ... Each worshipper of idols harbours hopes his special deities will give him more than other men possess. It does not really matter more of what; more beauty, more intelligence, more wealth, or even more affliction and more pain. And when one fails another takes its place, with hope of finding more of something else. Be not deceived by forms the "something" takes. An idol is a means for getting more." T-29.VIII.8

We decide we are not worthy of knowing God, so we pick an idol package instead. Looking at our choices as a package starts to lift our mind from the idea of linear time and scenarios, and into super-position, quantum, and potentialities, where we start to see that everything was decided before we even came to this world. Everything was a choice; we picked an idol package. However, there is no real cause-and-effect sequence going on in the idol package. And at some point we start to see that it has never brought us what we thought it would. Nemo got all of the things he said he would, and ended up lying face-down in a swimming pool!

Scene: Nemo's parents are divorced, and Nemo's mother and Anna's dad have been living together. Now they have separated and Anna and her father move to New York, leaving Nemo in deep despair.

Teenagers Nemo and Anna are in love and have been having a physical relationship for months in the home where they are living with Nemo's mother and Anna's father. When Anna is forced to move to New York, Nemo feels heartbroken. But, as the Course reminds us, we are never upset for the reason we think. All upsets can be traced back to the belief that we have separated from God. The feeling of loss was already in Nemo's mind before it played out in form.

This scene also demonstrates the projection of guilt onto bodies and behavior. The idea of two people splitting up, or one person leaving another, is seen as a bad thing. And as soon as something is judged as bad, fault comes in—the ego wants to know who will pay the price, who will take the blame. That is quite different from Jesus' teachings: "Let all things be exactly as they are" and "All things work together for good." W-268 and T-4.V.1 These teachings are holistic. Everything is perfect as it is; everything is happening as it must. This doesn't refer to the illusion of sequencing events on a one-way timeline; it refers to simultaneity, where there is no blame and nothing is good or bad. "You have to take the good with the bad" is a common expression. But the truth is that we don't have to take either because they are both ego judgments; they are both false interpretations.

Whether to stay or leave seems to be a big decision if we're with a partner. But all decisions are the same illusion; they are a choice for nothingness. If the ego has an attachment to the person, it's going to want the "stay" illusion; if it has an aversion to the person, it's going to want to the "leave" illusion. Through following Guidance, however, we can reach a point of non-attachment where it is possible to say, "I love you whether you stay or go" because True Love has no attachment, no investment in outcomes.

To the ego, that is ridiculous; it demands tangible goals. But what about peace of mind as a goal? Why not have a state-of-mind goal instead of a form-based goal? Peace of mind is perfectly attainable, but there is never an outcome in form that can truly satisfy. In fact, the Course says that our will is universal, and cannot be content with form of any kind.

Scene: *After years of searching for Anna, Nemo runs into her at a train station. They reunite and Anna tells Nemo she has always loved him. She gives him her phone number on a slip of paper and tells him to call her in two days. Rain falls onto the slip of paper with the number and it is no longer legible. Nemo goes to the boardwalk by the water every day and waits, but Anna doesn't appear.*

There's a line in the *Course* where Jesus says, "When you decide upon the form of what you want, you lose the understanding of its purpose." T-30.III.2 This is played out in the movie in terms of the relationship between Nemo and Anna. Nemo waiting for Anna every day at the boardwalk is an extreme example of being attached to a specific outcome in form. He has decided that being with Anna is the only thing that will make him happy. The words to the song "Mr. Sandman," which plays throughout the movie, describe perfectly how we ask for specifics in the hope that they will make us happy.

Mr. Sandman, bring me a dream
Make him the cutest that I've ever seen
Give him two lips like roses and clover
Then tell him that his lonesome nights are over.
Sandman, I'm so alone
Don't have nobody to call my own
Please turn on your magic beam
Mr. Sandman, bring me a dream.

The Chordettes, "Mister Sandman"

When we ask Mr. Sandman—the ego—to bring us a dream, we are asking for trouble! That is because a sense of lack and incompleteness lies beneath every request we make for an outcome in form. Happiness in form will never satisfy us. We can only be satisfied with content. Workbook Lesson 101 states, "God's Will for me is perfect happiness." But when we decide on which form is best—for example, the form of Anna or even the generic form that is "the cutest that I've ever seen"—we are no longer in touch with our universal will; we no longer know that our will and God's Will are the same.

Scene: A reporter who has sneaked into Nemo's hospital room is trying to make some sense of Nemo's life. He asks him, "Did you go with your mother or your father? Which girl did you marry?"

Nemo, who is a very old man, is looking back on the scenarios of his life. But he is extremely confused because there are so many and they seem to be from several lifetimes. The reporter, who wants answers that Nemo can't give, doesn't understand that all of the situations are purely hypothetical. At one point in the movie, he says to Nemo, "Did Elise die or didn't she? You can't have had children and *not* had them!"

But the movie shows the many possibilities that seem to be life in this world. Nemo chose the hypothetical situation of living with his mother; he also chose the hypothetical situation of staying with his father. He had three marriage scenarios at the same church. There was no particular plot or linear element stringing Nemo's life together.

But nothing happens by chance. The Course says, "I am responsible for what I see. I choose the feelings I experience, and I decide upon the goal I would achieve. And everything that seems to happen to me I ask for, and receive as I have asked." T-21.II.2 The Course also says, "It is impossible that anything should come to me unbidden by myself. Even in this world, it is I who rule my destiny. What happens is what I desire. What does not occur is what I do not want to happen." W-253 When we put those passages together; there's no wiggle room for blame, mistreatment, or abuse. Every scenario in Nemo's life brought him something that he wanted, even when what he seemed to experience was extremely painful or scary.

The ego would have us believe that our fears are form-based; such as the fear of drowning, or losing the one that we love. However, the fear that plays out over our lifetimes is actually the fear of Love, the fear of God. We project it out onto the world because it is intolerable to our mind. But the fearful scenarios, like all of the other scenarios, are unreal.

Jesus states in the Course, "What you seem to waken to is but another form of this same world you see in dreams. All your time is spent in dreaming. Your sleeping and your waking dreams have different forms, and that is all. Their content [the wish to change reality] is the same." T-18.II.5:11-14

Some people question the validity of Gary Renard's book *The Disappearance of the Universe*, where he claimed that two beings, Arten and Pursah, had visited him on his couch in Maine. Similar questions have been raised about Marlo Morgan's book *Mutant Message Down Under*, where Morgan went on a walkabout with Aborigines and described telepathic experiences. A controversy arose—did it really happen? And then Jimmy Twyman wrote a book, *Emissaries of Light*, where he described a silent brotherhood in Kosovo. Again, a controversy arose about whether or not his experience had actually occurred.

When Gary and I talked about whether or not Arten and Pursah were real or fictional, I said that the whole world is fictional. We try to make distinctions between what actually happened and what is fantasy or make-believe, but the truth is that it is *all* make-believe.

It's pointless to try and draw lines between what really happened and what didn't happen. All images and memories are fiction because they are made up by the ego; they are all equally false. Recognizing this is the only way to be happy. In *Mr. Nobody*, there is no answer to which scenarios are actually happening and which ones are not because all of them are Nemo's imagination.

Scene: Nemo has carved "yes" on one side of a coin, and "no" on the other.

Nemo has decided to make all of his decisions based on a flip of the coin. But what we do comes from what we think, and when our thinking is confused, we don't know who we are. Then it doesn't matter whether we think we're consciously choosing and the circumstances play out, or whether we think we're just leaving it to chance and the circumstances play out. It's the same thing. The world reflects what we think and believe. There is no such thing as chance; there are no accidents. Everything results from a decision in mind. "A decision is a conclusion based on everything you believe." T-24.In.2

This scene in the movie demonstrates how pointless it is trying to make sense of choices. It shows the futility of putting so much energy into hypotheticals. The ego mind thinks it can judge good decisions from bad decisions, advances from retreats, and gains from losses. But this movie illustrates that all decisions are the same. Nemo makes many of them in his various life scenarios, and all of them end up with him unhappy, suicidal, or dead. That is because all choices dictated by the ego keep us identified with duality and multiplicity.

What we must come to realize is that there is only one decision that needs to be made—that of choosing the Holy Spirit instead of the ego. Although this still seems to be a choice, it is a higher order of choice, and the only one that's going to get us out of the illusion. *A Course in Miracles* teaches that only the decisions we make with the Holy Spirit will unwind us from the maze of multiplicity and duality. We can call this choice atonement, correction, salvation, redemption, or whatever we want. It is the only real choice because it doesn't involve choosing between the images of the world. Instead, it is a choice to align our mind with the Holy Spirit, that we may accept ourselves as God created us.

We must be willing to have our minds returned to holistic thinking. We can't find the truth in the parts because they don't contain the whole; the whole transcends the parts. Holistic thinking is thinking in alignment with God. Trying to think in terms of threads, parts, and specifics is trying to think against God.

It's so simple! All we have to do is make one decision. One decision! If we could even faintly grasp what peace and rest and joy will result from the only decision that we need ever make, we would not wait a minute longer to make it.

Scene: Nemo starts to receive clear Guidance in the world of form— through words in the reflection of a mirror, specific instructions with his name on them in a newspaper, and a huge phone number displayed on a hill.

Nemo, who has always made his own choices, or left them to "chance," is now starting to see another way. His Guidance is becoming extremely clear, and instead of making decisions himself, Nemo now follows Spirit without questioning.

The direction he is given takes him to a dilapidated house that is full of dirt and has cats living in it. That Guidance would lead Nemo to such a place seems to make no sense to the logical mind. But when Nemo enters the house, he finds a big television set. When he turns it on, he sees himself at age 117. He has a conversation with his future self, and old Nemo tells adult Nemo that he must stay alive until February 12, 2092, at 5:50 a.m.

Scene: Old Nemo is once again talking to the reporter from his hospital bed.

The reporter says to Nemo, "Everything you say is contradictory. You can't have been in one place and another at the same time." Nemo replies, "You mean to say we have to make choices." The reporter says,

"Of all those lives, which one is the right one?" Nemo answers, "Each of these lives is the right one. Everything could have been anything else and it would have had just as much meaning."

The reporter persists, "You can't be dead and still be here. You can't not exist. Is there life after death?" Nemo cackles with laughter at the question. He says to the reporter, "After death! How can you be so sure you even exist? You don't exist. Neither do I. We live only in the imagination of a nine-year-old child. We are imagined by a nine-year-old child faced with an impossible choice."

This is the point in the movie where Nemo understands that he didn't mess anything up. He finally realizes that none of his life scenarios were real, that they all existed only in the imagination of a confused nine-year-old boy who was searching for love among a myriad of hypotheticals—hypotheticals of his mom, his dad, Anna, Elise, Jean, and all of his life scenarios. All along, he was searching to find the solution to the riddle of how he could have to make a choice between his parents. He couldn't understand it because it's not understandable. How can Love require us to make a choice? If Love is Oneness, then it doesn't have parts. It's whole; it's complete; it's everything. Why would everything force us to choose between something? It doesn't make any sense.

The last remaining freedom we have as prisoners of this world is our power to choose the Holy Spirit instead of the ego. All it takes is readiness on our part and willingness to have miracles performed through us, and Jesus will arrange time and space for us. Time is literally in the hands of the miracle worker.

Scene: *Nemo is in the hospital playing chess. He says that sometimes the only viable move is not to move.*

Nemo takes the reporter over to the window and they watch as the buildings of the city seem to crumble and fall. Nemo says, "The child is taking it apart. He doesn't need it anymore. Before, he was unable to make a choice because he didn't know what would happen. Now that he knows what will happen, he's unable to make a choice."

As he speaks, there is a flashback to the train station, where the child Nemo had to make his impossible choice. This time, however, Nemo runs away from the tracks and heads down a beautiful pathway leading into the forest. He picks up a leaf and blows it up into the air; the leaf travels through the forest, and eventually flutters across a chalk circle that has been drawn on the boardwalk pier overlooking the water. Just as the leaf crosses the circle, Anna steps into it. Nemo, who is lying on a bench a few feet away, opens his eyes and sees her.

This is what happens when we finally realize that we don't have to choose, when we let Spirit make the choice for us—the symbol of Love appears. When Nemo decided not to move—that is, when he decided not to make a choice in form at the train station and simply walked away instead—he was reunited with Anna, who symbolized True Love.

This is reminiscent of the "I Need Do Nothing" section in the Course, where Jesus says, "Now you need but to remember you need do nothing. It would be far more profitable now merely to concentrate on this than to consider what you should do." T-18.VII.5.6 He goes on to say, "Save time for me by only this one preparation, and practice doing nothing else. 'I need do nothing' is a statement of allegiance, a truly undivided loyalty. Believe it for just one instant, and you will accomplish more than is given to a century of contemplation, or of struggle against temptation." T-18.7.6.6-8

This means that we can simply review what has already gone by, making no attempt to change or fix or rearrange the images of the script. We no longer need to seek to change the dream, but simply to change our mind about the dream. It is very relaxing to remember that by ourselves we can do nothing, but with the Holy Spirit we can do all things.

Scene: *Nemo, the old man, is in the hospital, dying. A drone camera is recording it all, and huge screens on buildings around the huge, futuristic city are showing his last moments.*

Although Nemo is dying, he has a smile full of peace and happiness on his face. This is symbolic of the freedom we experience when we finally let go of the choices of the world. Nemo's last words are, "This is the most beautiful day of my life. Anna."

This scene reminds me of something in Ken Wapnick's book *Absence from Felicity.* Jesus asked Helen Schucman, "What do you do when you find yourself in a desert?" She hesitated and he asked again. When she didn't come up with the answer, he finally gave it to her, "Leave." With Workbook Lesson 128, "The world I see holds nothing that I want," Jesus is calling the mind into the stillness in which we leave the choices of the world.

Not choosing in form frees us to let go of all the wrong-minded choices of the world and decide instead for right-mindedness. When we let the Holy Spirit decide for us, all conflict is eliminated. We no longer need to try and change or control the images of the illusory world because we recognize that we are observing something that has already happened. When we no longer plan, scheme, or strain to try and make things work out the way we want them to, a sense of effortlessness comes in. There is no longer a need to look back and say, "This should have been different."

Scene: As Nemo is lying dead in the hospital bed, the clock flips over to 5:50 am. It is February 12, 2092.

In the very next moment, the clock turns back to 05:49 and time seems to start to reverse. Leaves blow back up in the air, rain falls upward into the sky, and the smoke goes back into Nemo's father's cigarette. *This illustration of time seeming to move backwards is symbolic of the mind returning to the moment it believed separation from God was possible, and reversing that decision.* With a gasp, Nemo comes back to life—that is, he accepts the Atonement. He begins to laugh and laugh, demonstrating the promise Jesus makes to us in the Course: "The world will end in laughter."

Love is who we are. Love is One. Love does not have parts; it is whole. It is complete. It is everything. As Nemo learned in *Mr. Nobody,* it doesn't make sense that Love would require a choice between two things. When it seems as though there are choices to be made, it is exciting to ask for Guidance, to ask, "What is this for? What is most helpful in this seeming situation?" We can go in a new direction now by listening for and following that Guidance. Our prayer to the Holy Spirit can be, "When there are choices to be made, I want You to make them. I want Your decisions to unwind me from time and space." It's a gentle and gradual process.

Many people are familiar with the Serenity Prayer: "God grant me the serenity to accept the things I cannot change, the courage to change the things I can, and the wisdom to know the difference." Another way to state this is, "Seek not to change the world, but choose to change your mind about the world." T-21.In.1

Both are telling us that we do not need to try and fix anything in form. As the Bible says in Corinthians, we are looking through a darkened glass. It is only our filter of judgment and interpretation that needs to be cleaned. Our cleared and transparent mind is the gateway back to eternity.

An invaluable teaching of this movie is that we no longer have to waste any more time on hypotheticals or on meaningless choices. We no longer have to indulge in "coulda-shoulda-woulda" thinking. What a relief and a release to finally see the futility of it all! What a gift to know that we don't have to try and figure anything out! We can finally relax.

Chapter 4

THERE ARE NO
PROBLEMS IN QUANTUM

It can be suffocating and depressing to feel locked into a lifetime. The Course took me into complete disillusionment. It says that all the roadways of the world lead to death, and that men have died upon seeing this. That is a pretty depressing thought. But Jesus goes on to say that if they had just taken their next step, they could have been led on to heights of happiness. Something lifted in my heart when I read that. Heights of happiness! We can start to gain an appreciation for disillusionment when we recognize that disillusionment is the forerunner to heights of happiness.

I am convinced that there are no problems. When someone presents a problem, it's fun to see what is going to happen. The no-problem state of mind is very joyful. Heaven knows there is nothing attractive about any specific form, but there is a Presence underneath that is joyful, loving, and laughing. We are attracted to that laughter. That is why everyone enjoys comedy; because there is a deeper Presence behind the laughter that we would like to experience. If something seems joyful, happy, or peaceful, and we are drawn to it, then we are more willing to move toward it in our mind. When children find something they enjoy, they learn it and retain it in memory. It is the same with spirituality—we need to be drawn in. It must be more than a lot of rituals and practices.

We can come to the experience of awakening by way of different symbols, but ultimately the experience is about Love. I have met people from many walks of life—different cultures, different languages, different countries—but the experience is always about Love. *Everything* is ultimately about Love! It doesn't matter what we have strived or worked for; it doesn't matter how we have conceptualized this world.

After much reading and experimenting I found a deep resonance with *A Course in Miracles*. I had a strong feeling that I was to use it and go deep, that I was not to skim the surface anymore. An inner Presence seemed to be saying, "Pick this one and apply it." I had a feeling of destiny, as though it was all part of a pre-arranged plan. I felt as though I had already done this in form and I was just reliving it, thinking I was choosing something new and different. Jesus says in the Course that we do not even pick the form of the curriculum; it takes that much surrender. The Course leads us through a washing and rinsing of all that is not love. We must be willing to go through as many cycles as it takes to clear the altar of the mind.

I feel that the spiritual journey is one-percent principle and ninety-nine percent practice. When we take a non-dualistic pathway like *A Course in Miracles* and start to apply it in our day-to-day, moment-to-moment experience of living, it can feel like a pretty sharp jolt. Sometimes it seems like the rug is being pulled out from under us. But I came to see that application of the Course was exciting and that I really wanted it.

The key to my ability to transfer the training and to awaken to joy and happiness was the practice of making no exceptions to Jesus' teachings to anything in my life. Jesus wrote an owner's manual for waking up, and I fully committed myself to following his instructions with diligence and persistence. I had a feeling that this would save me an enormous amount of time. The ego may have thought otherwise, but I found it exhilarating.

The ego always wants to add something on. It wants to throw in an "and" when the sentence ends with a period. I have heard many people say, "I know the world is an illusion, but ..." and it does not matter what follows the "but," because the "but" contradicts the first part of the sentence. Jesus would end that sentence with a period. When we consistently apply the teachings of the Course, we start to gain the joy and confidence of the Spirit. We start being able to bring light and peace to everyone and to every situation because we realize there is nothing we have to avoid.

When we are turning from upside-down to right-side-up thinking—realizing that cause is in the mind, that the projected world comes from within us—Spirit convinces us that we are on the right path by providing us with a lot of loving symbols. They are needed because, although it is possible to make a quick turn in the mind, it is quite rare. Generally, we need lots of evidence and witnesses to show us that it is safe. The miracle sees the false as false. "It merely looks on devastation, and reminds the mind that what it sees is false." W-pII.13.1 That is why we are called upon to be consistently miracle-minded. Jesus says the appropriate use of denial is to deny the belief that error can hurt us. This is the transformation that we are giving ourselves over to.

We are loosening from the idea that there is an objective world. The early Course Workbook lessons show us that the thoughts we think we think, and the world we think we see, are identical. Workbook Lesson 15 states, "My thoughts are images that I have made." This means that the world is not outside the mind. We are completely dealing with mind; it is never a question of dealing with behaviors.

If there is a speaking component, it is under Christ's control. We allow ourselves to be spoken through, and oftentimes there is nothing to say. We definitely do not need to tell someone that it's all an illusion. Occasionally we might be guided to smile, hug somebody, or put our arm around somebody. Those things come in naturally when we are in alignment with Spirit. We are not called to give discourses on the unreality of the world, especially when we are out in public. We are not called to say that we are Jesus Christ in the middle of the Bible belt. We often try to get ahead of ourselves, to jump from A to Z, because there is something inside us that wants it to be over fast. We think that saying the right words will magically resolve everything, but that is not the way it goes. It is not about trying.

Jesus states in the Course, "I need do nothing" T-18.VII.6 However, this is true only when we have attained that still point in our mind where the doer—the one whose value comes from doing—disappears. We cannot skip over what is practical. We cannot say, "Well, the Course says I am not a body and I need do nothing, so I am checking out." That misses the point. Jesus tells us that "An untrained mind can accomplish nothing" W-In.1 As long as we need mind training, we have to be practical. We have to be guided to do certain things and not to do others as we are unwinding from the world.

Jesus says in the Course that we are here to correct the error from the bottom up. This means that we are to join with the Holy Spirit and to bring the illusions, all the scraps of ego that are in the mind, to the light. Jesus says to bring the illusion to the Truth, not the Truth to the illusion. That would be trying to correct error from the top down. Jesus took the time to show that none of the beliefs that built this world have any reality. The real teaching was his demonstration of being the Presence. Without that, we wouldn't even know about Jesus; he would have been dismissed in his day as merely some whacko who said that our sins are forgiven. Jesus' teachings were powerful directions to correct the error from the bottom up. I am here to do the same thing; to share the message of True Healing, which requires bringing the illusion to the Truth.

I love how practical it is. I call it practically joyful. That is why I am happy to witness to you how it seemed to go for me, because it offers a sense of, "If he can do it, I can do it." We have the same Guide.

Chapter 5

SOURCE CODE

Key Themes

- Quantum Love
- Accepting True Purpose

Movie Synopsis

U.S. Army helicopter pilot Captain Colter Stevens wakes up to find himself on a commuter train to Chicago, at 7:40 a.m. He is seated opposite a woman named Christina Warren, who knows him by the name Sean Fentress. He doesn't seem to know her and appears uncertain of his own identity. His last memory is of flying on a mission in Afghanistan. As he comes to grips with this revelation, the train explodes, killing everyone aboard.

He awakens to find himself strapped inside a metal capsule. From a computer screen, Air Force Captain Colleen Goodwin tells him that he actually is Colter and that he is now on a mission from inside the capsule to locate the maker of a bomb that destroyed a train headed into Chicago. He has been plugged into Source Code, a time-loop program that allows him to take over someone's body in a re-enactment of their last eight minutes of life.

Colter is sent into Source Code repeatedly as Sean Fentress in the final minutes aboard the train before it explodes. Colter is about to embark on the journey of a lifetime. He will come to see that nothing is as it appears. Everything that he thinks he knows about time and space will start to be dismantled in a rapid way. He is not who he thinks he is and nothing seems to be under his conscious control. He comes to see that everything is going to be okay, that he can rest and trust in a higher purpose for his life.

Introduction

This movie is an express train into the Abstract. We are actually going into consciousness. Consciousness is our laboratory, our classroom. The world is not our classroom, consciousness is. We will experience this through *Source Code*, an amazing quantum movie given to us by the Holy Spirit.

Source Code is a quantum love story. Colter and Christina will have a series of brief holy encounters where it is obvious that Christina really likes Colter, even though she is surprised because the person that she knows as Sean is different from the way that he was. There is something about him that is fresh and spontaneous. Colter is going to have a series of shocking experiences as he starts to see that the person that he *thinks* he is, he is not. He is going to start to realize that he doesn't have a clue about what is going on, that he has been wrong about everything. Colter and Christina both symbolize the journey of being taken into an experience of quantum love.

This movie is an opportunity to see that we have no idea what will make us happy. And it has a delightful destination. When the Spirit takes the lead, we do not know what is happening, but it is always for our own best interests.

David's Movie Commentary

Scene: *A man is asleep on a train. Sounds of a helicopter and military commands are faintly heard. He startles awake. The woman seated opposite addresses him in a familiar manner as Sean. He is quite disoriented. He tells her that he doesn't know who she is and that his name is Captain Colter Stevens, a helicopter pilot.*

In this scene, Colter doesn't know what is going on. He looks in the bathroom mirror on the train and sees a face that he doesn't recognize. He looks in his wallet and is shocked to see a different identity. He has an encounter with a woman he does not know and is quite perplexed. He is frustrated because the situation is not meeting his expectations of being Captain Colter Stevens. He is looking around as if he is thinking, *This is not my Captain Colter scenario at all.*

In one sense, this is how the journey goes. This movie is like an LSD trip without the drug to loosen the mind. If we think we already know who we are in our everyday perceptions of ourselves, the Holy Spirit has a lot of work to do to unwind our mind from the grip of this idea. We might have some mystical experiences that show us we are not who we think we are. But as soon as we come back from these expansive experiences, the ego will try to dismiss them by saying, *That can't possibly be who you are.* If we seem unable to regain that expansive state, there is the temptation to think, *OK, I'll just resign myself to being the human being that I think I am.*

Scene: *The train explodes. There is a flash of light and Sean finds himself in a dark capsule. A woman's voice addresses him as Captain Colter Stevens. He is very confused. She asks him to report what happened. She appears in military uniform on a video screen. She runs him through some exercises to refresh his memory, after which he recalls that her name is Goodwin. Colter asks to speak to his father. She responds by asking him, "Who bombed the train, Captain?" He doesn't know. She tells him, "Go back and try again. You'll have eight minutes, same as last time. Start with the bomb. Where is it? What does it look like? Find the bomb and you'll find the bomber." With a blast of light, Colter is back in the same seat on the train.*

The first time Colter showed up on the train, he was extremely disoriented. Now Goodwin has given him a purpose, and her guidance gives him a clearer focus. The scenario starts to reflect his mind— Colter finds the bomb hidden in the ceiling above the restroom on board the train.

We may think we know who we are, where we live, and what our history is. But we don't. We are asleep and dreaming. We think we are one of the dream characters; we have forgotten the divinity of who we are. Certain characters and situations show up repeatedly in our life, not unlike the train scenarios. For Colter, it's an eight-minute slice of time on a ride into Chicago, where the train blows up.

This is a dream world where we are a make-believe dream character that God did not create and does not know about. We are lost, wandering in time and space, trying to make the best of it. We do not know what the meaning of life is because if we did, this world would disappear; we would be back home in Heaven. Since we do not know the meaning of life, we are confused. We try to keep our head above water, we try to make it through the day, but really we do not know what is happening.

Colter is going through a series of experiences that are going to dislodge his mind from everything he thinks he knows. This is how the spiritual journey goes. As we go deeper down the rabbit hole, everything we thought we knew disappears. The more insights and mystical experiences we have, the more everything keeps shifting. Things keep falling away because the lesson, the purpose, underneath this whole dream, is forgiveness. We must empty our mind of everything we think we think, and think we know about our identity so that our real Identity can be revealed to us by Spirit.

Scene: *Colter arrives back in the capsule a second time. He is angry and distressed and demands to be briefed on what is happening. Goodwin tells him that he's been with them for two months, that he is not in a simulation and that lives are depending on him, as a second bombing attack is imminent. Colter tells her where he found the bomb and that it has a cell phone detonator. Goodwin instructs him to concentrate on the passengers in his car, get to know them, narrow the suspect pool and look for the ones who seem quiet, withdrawn or nervous. "As always, you'll have eight minutes," says Goodwin. "Then I blow up again?" asks Colter. "Yes," says Goodwin. He starts to ask about his father again as they send him back onto the train.*

Colter does not understand the deeper meaning of his experiences yet, but with the purpose of finding the bomber, he becomes friendly with the young woman, Christina, who is sitting across from him. She starts to talk about moving to India and looking for a guru. It seems as though she is looking for the meaning of life, but she is a reflection of Colter's mind. It is Colter who is looking for the meaning of life, and this is symbolized by him meeting a woman who is talking about finding herself.

In this world we like to follow the plot, to think we know what is happening, what is coming next. But these great quantum movies are like spiritual experiences. They start to dismantle the world as we know it, and we find ourselves knowing less and less about what is happening. We do not have to know; there is a Presence behind all this that knows what It is doing. Instead of feeling nervous when things start to dismantle and fall apart, we can accept that we personally do not know, and see it as a good thing.

Scene: Colter asks Christina, the woman across from him, to play a "game" with him of finding suspicious passengers on the train. When Colter sees a man he thinks might be the bomber, he impulsively kisses Christina, then tells her that he has a bad feeling about the train and that she should get off with him, which she does. Colter follows the man, attacks him, and ends up falling onto the train tracks.

This is how perception works: the world and the characters perceived are the result of what is going on in our consciousness. By focusing on something, when we have a purpose in mind, we draw it to us. The world is seen through the lens of that purpose. In this scene, Colter sees a man who is sweating and looking unwell come out of the restroom. He thinks the man is the bomber.

We can notice in our own life that whatever we pursue or whatever goals we have, the purpose determines what we perceive. As long as there are ego—or self-concept—purposes, variable outcomes will be the result. Some will be judged as good, some as bad, but none of them are forgiveness. There is a higher purpose for the whole scenario, and that is to forgive and to find love. That purpose is always present, but because it is not out front, it is not yet in awareness.

Colter is coming into purpose in his eight-minute segments. Imagine what it would be like if we woke up every day with the purpose of forgiveness: *Today is a new day and I'm going to use it for forgiveness. I'm going to keep the purpose of forgiveness out front, and I'm going to perceive everything and everyone who comes to me as helping me to achieve my goal of forgiveness, because it is that important to me.*

That is what the mind training of *A Course in Miracles* is about: holding a loving purpose, a peaceful purpose, a joyful purpose out front. And then the day will reflect that purpose back to us. The "Rules for Decision" section in the Course says, "If I make no decisions by myself, this is the day that will be given me." T-30.I.4.2 As long as we are in flow with the harmony of the universe—with peace, love, and joy—we will perceive a peaceful world. Until that happens there will be situations and events that do not seem to make a lot of sense, but that is only because the mind does not yet understand what its real purpose is. This is the case with Colter. He is doing his best, but he does not see the healing or the greater purpose.

It is clear that Colter is beginning to like Christina. He tells her that she is kind, decent and real. Although she still thinks he is Sean Fentress, Christina is beginning to see something different in him that she really likes. Clearly, there is a spark between them.

Scene: *Laying on the train track, Colter is hit by a train and finds himself back in the capsule, which is becoming cold and frosty. He has also lost communication with Goodwin and he begins to panic. When communication is regained he meets Rutledge, who is the inventor of Source Code, and for the first time he is told that he's in Source Code. He asks what happens after the eight minutes on the train. Rutledge says, "Nothing. You cease to exist inside the train. You cannot exist inside Source Code beyond Sean Fentress's last eight minutes."*

These scenes will show more and more clearly that what we perceive is what we believe. Colter perceives himself as being in a capsule, where the power has gone out and it is dark and cold; he feels alone and is afraid for his life. But it is not the capsule and the conditions that are making him feel that way. We believe things happen in the world—that there are conditions or situations that make us feel alone, trapped, afraid, or desperate—but the world does not make us feel anything. What we feel in our mind and our consciousness, we then project onto the world. So the environment that we perceive is a projection of thoughts, beliefs, and feelings in mind. What we believe, we perceive.

In Lesson 189 of *A Course in Miracles* Jesus says, "You will look upon that which you feel within." Colter is feeling trapped, helpless, and powerless, and so he perceives himself in a world where the power has gone off. He doesn't have a context for anything, and he is afraid.

On the spiritual journey, we may be tempted to get frightened when we do not have a larger context. Unwanted things seem to be happening, but they are a reflection of what is going on in our mind. We perceive what we believe and that is what makes this world seem terrifying sometimes. The unconscious belief system is quite dark, and the dreams and dream symbols that represent it will seem to manifest.

These eight-minute segments can be thought of as little incarnations. Some say that karma is behind reincarnation. But who created karma? The ego cannot create; it was not given creative abilities. Only God and the creations of God have creative abilities. So reincarnation does not have a cause. But if there is a *belief* in karma, or the unconscious, or guilt, then the scenarios seem to play out. We do not know how they started or how we got there.

We see that Colter is having a series of perceptual experiences. That is exactly what is going on in our own lives; even the room in which we seem to be sitting is a perceptual experience that is coming from a set of beliefs. If we believe that spirituality is important, we may seem to find ourselves in a room reading a book about strange movies, and wondering if this will lead somewhere. But the whole scenario is just a reflection of belief system. We can imagine it as a motion picture; that is what it is.

Scene: *Back on the train, Colter wants to find out what is going on. He asks Christina to use the Internet on her phone to look up a "friend" who is in the military, a Captain Colter Stevens. A few minutes later, she tells him that Captain Colter Stevens was killed in action two months ago.*

Christina tells him that Captain Stevens died two months ago. As she speaks, a look of disbelief comes over Colter's face. Then he notices that Christina's face has taken on a dream-like quality. This is a clue that the scenario isn't real, that it is make-believe, just a movie set. Even though it seems like there are real people in a real world, Colter is starting to get a sense that everything is being generated from his mind, his consciousness.

Scene: Inside the capsule, Colter's first question is "Am I dead?" Goodwin eventually shares with him that part of his brain remains activated. He says, "What about the rest of me? I can see my hands and my feet, they still move" Goodwin explains, "They are a manifestation, they are just your way of making sense of all this." Colter asks, "Are you saying that I'm just imagining that I'm still alive, that I'm in this capsule?" At this point the whole capsule begins to expand.

Colter has just been told that he is imagining the conditions in the capsule. With even the suggestion that what he seems to be experiencing is not real, the tight little capsule suddenly expands. That is the power of the mind: the environment, the relationships, and the world we think we are in all start to shift. That is what happens to our perception as we start to let go of limiting beliefs about who we are, when we start to question that we are limited to being a person occupying a tiny coordinate in time and space inside a cosmos that seems to be outside of us.

Mystical experiences reveal that everything we perceive is just as we think it is. The entire world is subjective. There is no objective world outside of consciousness; there is nothing observed that is apart from the observer. Colter has just had his first mystical moment.

Scene: After the capsule expands, Goodwin asks him what happened. "I asked you a question," says Colter, "Where am I?" When Goodwin says "That's classified," he yells at her. Military Commander Rutledge then joins Goodwin and begins addressing Colter directly.

Rutledge tells Colter, "This may be difficult for you to hear, but you are a hand on a clock. We set you, you move forward; we reset you, you move again. That represents the entirety of your function here." Rutledge tells him that many soldiers would find Colter's situation— the opportunity to continue serving their country—preferable to death. Colter comments that any soldier he served with would say one death was service enough. Rutledge says "Fine, you can have that in return for completing this mission. I'll give you what you want, terminate your service, let you die."

There is an arrogance in what Rutledge says to Colter. We can see Goodwin's reaction to it on her face as she is listening to this "military intelligence." It appears as though part of her is disturbed by her job, by her commander, by that thought system. She is starting to question the simple following of orders and commands.

Rutledge does not show value or respect for Colter's choice or life. He may understand a little bit about Source Code, but he does not understand Source at all. He does not reflect the clarity and the Love of our Divine Source, which created us in Spirit.

Scene: *Colter is sent repeatedly into Source Code without a rest. Rutledge tells Colter, "We have to keep doing this until you find the bomber. I know you're exhausted, but we cannot fail. You can do this. You're a born hero, son, even your father thinks so. Saving people is what you do best."*

Rutledge plays an audio recording of Colter's father speaking about him after he died. Colter's father says, "It was his third tour. I didn't want him to go back. I just started feeling like he didn't want to come home anymore. Somehow he couldn't come home. He wouldn't talk to me, wouldn't hear me. Finally he said he just couldn't leave his unit out there without him. And that was that. Those guys were his family. I said some things I shouldn't have. I don't know. I never fully understood him and I can't believe he's gone."

Colter has said throughout the movie, "I need to speak with my dad." There is an unresolved relationship issue here between father and son, a grievance that is underneath the surface. Unkind words were exchanged, and communication was broken off. Colter feels the hurt of no longer having communication with his father, from not having been able to say good-bye. After all that Colter has been through, he is finally getting to the buried hurt and pain, which we all have and need to let go of. Colter has a regret with his father, which is interesting because we all have a regret with *our* Father. Lying in the capsule listening to his father's voice, Colter realizes that he can call his dad from the train and try to heal the relationship. He says to Rutledge, "Send me back in."

Scene: *Back on the train, Colter believes he has disarmed the bomb and having found the bomber, follows him off the train. The bomber shoots Colter, and then Christina, who had left the train in pursuit of Colter. The bomber drives off, leaving them lying in the parking lot, dying. They make eye contact and Colter says "Christina, stay with me. Everything is going to be okay, this isn't the end." Off in the distance, Colter sees the train explode.*

We see two bodies apparently dying, but they are making eye contact. This is the glimmer of the holy relationship. Love is in that eye contact. There is a sense that this is not the end, and that everything is going to be alright. We can feel the spark of love between them. His heart can be felt, even though he does not know whether he is Captain Colter or Sean Fentress, dead or alive. There is a loosening up and a spark is starting to come through.

Colter has finally figured out who the bomber is, but he is wondering what the point of all this is. In an earlier scene, Rutledge told him that it was to prevent a dirty bomb from exploding in Chicago, and that he will be a hero for letting his consciousness be used to save lives. But the True Purpose of Colter's experience is much deeper than that. Everything that seems to be happening is so that he can come into an experience of complete Forgiveness. That is what *all* of our lives are about: to learn that there is a much greater purpose than our little missions. This is an important assignment for Colter, and Christina is part of his wake-up dream.

Scene: *In the capsule again, Colter gives full details about the bomber's vehicle, which contains the nuclear device. A team is deployed and the bomber is captured before he detonates the second bomb. Colter says, "About our deal...." Rutledge responds, "I had hoped that you might reconsider that for the sake of the program." Colter responds, "I have. I want something else now. I still want to die. But I want to go back in* *and save all those people on that train first." Rutledge says, "It doesn't work that way. It can't." Colter says, "I know. I'm not really asking you to believe me, Sir. I'm asking you to have the decency to have me try."*

The military got what they wanted; they are satisfied that their program works. But we noticed during Colter's transitions to and from the train that he saw images, or memories, flash by. They were symbols of the faith in his mind, symbols of peace, love, and joy. He sees beyond what Rutledge can see. They are symbolic that the soul, the Spirit, is transcendent in him. All these memories are a hint that there is a higher purpose of light and healing. This is what *A Course in Miracles* calls the happy dream, or true perception, or the real world.

Scene: *As Rutledge and his colleagues celebrate finding the bomber, Goodwin sits quietly by the computer with Colter. He says, "He's not going to send me back in, is he Goodwin?" She tells him that she is still waiting for an answer." Colter says, "I missed something, Captain. That train shouldn't have blown up. There must've been a second detonator." Christina replies, "It's a computer program, Captain. All of those on the train are lost." He says, "I know, I get it, but you're just plain wrong." Goodwin responds, "Captain, Christina is dead." Colter says, "She doesn't have to be, Ma'am. I'm asking you to just send me back, then switch me off."*

Goodwin agrees to send him back in and says, "At the end of this Source Code, I will terminate your life support. There will be no coming back." He replies, "I'm going to save her, Goodwin." She replies, "It was an honor, Captain, and I thank you for your service." She sends him back to the train for the final time.

Colter asks Goodwin for one final eight-minute chance to go back on the train and save Christina. He believes that consciousness is contained in the brain. But it isn't. The brain is only a part of the projection and does not contain consciousness. That is the realization when the purpose is forgiveness and love.

There is a realization that there never was life in the characters, or life in the brain. It was all in our mind. When we forgive, we see that all the memories are reconfigured and that we are in all of the memories. More accurately, all of the memories are in us. Everything happens in the mind, not in the brain. Brain research attempts to show that the brain thinks. But the brain does not think. The electrical impulses and neurotransmitters are merely parts of the projection. Everything is in the mind, where it can be reconfigured by the Holy Spirit.

Scene: *With the desire to heal his relationship with his father, Colter calls him from the train, saying he is Sean Fentress, a friend who served in action with his son. He tells his father that he was there when Colter died and that Colter had told him that the last time they talked, it was tough, and he wanted to say that he was sorry. Colter's father tells him, "I loved him very much. I wish I could've told him that." Colter says "He knows it. Take care, Mr. Stevens."*

Colter then makes a bet with a passenger, who is a comedian, that he can't make everyone on the train laugh. Christina says to Colter, "What has gotten into you today? You're like a different person." "It's the new me," says Colter, "Look at all this." "What?" she asks. "All this life. What would you do if you knew you had less than a minute to live?" says Colter. "Make those seconds count," she replies. "I'd kiss you again," says Colter. "Again?" she manages to say before he kisses her right before the eight-minute point. The scene freezes, with everyone on the train laughing.

Colter has forgiven his dad. The key to happiness is realizing that nobody is ever doing anything wrong; they are reflecting only what we believe. If we see something that we do not like, we can let it go and remember our commitment for happiness, for love, for joy. We do not have to hold on to it; we do not have to harbor it.

In this scene, we see the laughter; we see the happiness on everyone's faces. Time is not what we think it is. This movie asks, "Where is my heart?" If our heart truly desires love and forgiveness, the whole world will reconfigure to the brightness and love in our mind. When we allow love to be the most important thing in our life, everything, all of time, will reconfigure. Jesus says that he will arrange time and space for us if we are willing to perform miracles.

Scene: *Back at the military facility, Goodwin unplugs Colter from Source Code and the freeze- frame ends. The eight minutes have ended and Colter and Christina have moved into a timeline beyond the eight-minute loop. Colter looks at his watch and says, "Everything's going to be okay!" They are walking through the city of Chicago, and Christina says, "Come here, I want to show you something." Colter stops as he sees the sculpture that he's seen so many times previously during his transitions from the train to the capsule. "Do you believe in fate?" he asks Christina. "Not really, I'm more of a dumb-luck kinda gal," she responds, "What do you want to do today?" "I think we should stay here for a while, this feels like exactly where we're supposed to be, doesn't it?" answers Colter.*

This is a great quantum movie that shows that form does not cause anything. Everything gets reconfigured, even memories. Colter frequently saw Christina in bright light during the transitions. The reason he asked her if she believed in fate was because he had to be willing to go for the light without holding back.

When we talk about the spiritual journey and about relationships, a word comes to mind—"commitment." It is an interesting word. I have had people in my life who have said, "I do not want to say the 'C' word." The C word is not cancer—it is commitment! For many, the word commitment brings up fear. What is the fear about? It is the fear of love, the fear of getting locked into something, the fear of being trapped. Jesus says in *A Course in Miracles* that the ego does not know what commitment is. The ego is impulsive; it does not know itself; it does not know what anything means. It is a puff of nothing. What would we expect from it? It thinks it knows a lot, but it is afraid of love and does not know what commitment is.

Jesus describes the Atonement, which is the way to wake up from this world, from this dream of separation, as a *total* commitment. Therefore, if the ego does not know what commitment is, and the Atonement is a total commitment, the direction becomes obvious. The Holy Spirit has to introduce the idea that all commitments in time and space are used as temporary commitments. That is why we have relationships, partnerships, and marriages. The Holy Spirit has to introduce commitment to start to train our mind in discipline, mind training, and purification. Ultimately this takes us all the way to our commitment to forgive, which is our commitment to know God.

Every relationship is a total commitment in terms of Purpose. The ego does not believe that and asks, "What does that mean? How could every relationship be a total commitment?" Purpose points us back to the mind. There is a Purpose underneath all our memories and images that unifies them and brings us back to God. At first Colter was committed to his mission to find the bomber, but then he became committed to a deeper purpose, when he started to fall in love. Near the end of the movie Christina said, "You are like a different person," because she could sense that Colter had a genuine commitment to something beyond himself. Beautiful, loving traits had started to come through him. He wanted to save her, and ultimately, to save the world.

We can use temporary commitments as stepping stones towards a full commitment to Peace of Mind. In a partnership, for example, we can commit to a Higher Purpose—that of making healing our top priority. The right use of relationship is learning to let go of expectations, cease trying to get something from our partner, or attempting to change them. As we release all of these ego projections, we can transfer that to everyone we meet.

That is how to come to agape love, to unconditional love. We have the same commitment to everyone. There is no hierarchy where we say, *OK, here are the important ones in my life, and there are the rest of the seven billion that I am indifferent about. If I see them coming, I will just walk right by them. Or do I have to smile?* Jesus says yes—they are all us, and they are all important. We have to learn to extend love to all of them. We have to send that same loving blessing because we need it. Committing to that extension of love is how to find out that *we* are loved.

Whatever we perceive in another person, whatever we find absolutely unacceptable, is something we believe in our own mind. They are simply acting it out for us. For example, if we perceive somebody as lazy, uncaring, or unintelligent, they are reflecting our own belief that this is possible. We have to believe it before we can perceive it; that is how projection works. We try to disown it and think, *Oh, I am not like that at all and I cannot be around that.* But when we leave one partner for a different one, the same things that bothered us before are going to get reflected right back again. They could take the form of rejection, abandonment, or anything else that has been an ongoing pattern in our life.

When we become aware of our thought patterns, we can start to feel gratitude for our partner. We can thank them for showing us our unhealed places. As we start to realize that people are not doing anything to us, we become more aware, our consciousness starts to expand. When we realize that we are doing it to ourselves in consciousness, we can stop it. We do not have to hold on to the old thought patterns any more.

Our Purpose is awareness. Like Captain Colter, we may not know exactly who we are, we may find ourselves in different environments, but we choose to be attentive. The greatest gift from all of this is a sense of gratitude. That is what forgiveness does.

Scene: *Colter sends Goodwin an email telling her the bomber was caught and that if she's reading the email, Source Code works better than she or Rutledge ever imagined. He writes, "You thought you were creating eight minutes of a past event, but you weren't. You created a whole new world! If I'm right, you have a Captain Colter Stevens somewhere at the Source Code facility, waiting to be sent on a mission. Promise me you'll help him and when you do, do me a favor and tell him… everything's going to be okay."*

If we truly believed the message of Source Code, if we knew that we couldn't change anything, we could just rest. We have the power right now to rest deeply, to let go of all the pursuits, all attempts to make ourselves better. Everything's going to be okay because everything *is* okay. Colter wanted to save Christina and ultimately, to save the world—and he did. But he didn't do it by changing anything in form; he did it by accepting complete Forgiveness in his mind. Our mind is that powerful! What a spectacular movie!

Chapter 6

SOLARIS

True Forgiveness

We always make the best decision we can based upon what we believe in that moment. When I was growing up, my father and I experienced a lot of tension with each other for many years. He had bipolar disorder and it was very difficult for him. As I got older and went through my transformation of consciousness and really forgave him—and forgave myself and forgave the world—my father started showing up in my awareness as an angel. He got happier and happier and our relationship began to improve. People would say, "Your dad has really changed a lot," and I would say, "My mind has really changed." My father was just reflecting that back. In fact, he came to me one day and said, "David, I'm sorry. I was not a very good father. I didn't do the things that a good father should do."

I replied, "Nonsense! I don't believe that for one instant. You did the best you could and I did the best I could. You didn't let me down and I didn't let you down. We're not going to buy into that guilt trip anymore."

He lit up when I said this. His whole demeanor changed and he instantly reflected love back to me. That simple exchange completely rearranged our view of everything that had taken place during those early years. None of it mattered anymore. We had been mistaken about many things because we couldn't perceive truly while we were going through our time together.

All that had really been happening was that I had tried to hold him to the "father role," and he had tried to hold me to the "son role." This created a wrestling match that led to untrue beliefs like, "You should be a better father," and "You should be a better son."

When we finally let go, he was no longer my father, and I was no longer his son. We recognized our perfect equality in that moment, and only the love was left. We laughed and hugged each other. We shared an intense joy together. The war was over. From that instant on, we were happy when we were together, right up to the point when he passed away.

Key Themes

- True Forgiveness
- Accepting Our Innocence

Movie Synopsis

Solaris centers on psychologist Dr. Chris Kelvin, who is approached by emissaries for DBA, a corporation that is operating a space station orbiting the planet Solaris. They relay a video message sent from Chris's scientist friend Dr. Gibarian, in which he requests that Kelvin come to the station to help solve an unusual phenomenon that is happening on board the ship. He is unwilling to explain more, but tells Chris that although the obvious solution would be to leave, none of the astronauts want to return home. Chris agrees to a solo mission to Solaris as a last attempt to bring the crew home safely. Upon arriving at the space station, Chris learns that Gibarian has committed suicide and most of the crew have either died or disappeared under bizarre circumstances. Both surviving crew members, Snow and Dr. Gordon, are reluctant to explain the situation at hand.

As the movie progresses, however, it becomes clear that what is happening on board the space station is that the unhealed thoughts of the crew members are manifesting in forms, called visitors, which seem terrifying and unbelievable. Chris begins to have the same experience. As the space station gets closer and closer to Solaris, his own unhealed thoughts and beliefs are brought to the surface, forcing Chris to reexamine many of his deeply held concepts. With the profoundly healing power of Solaris leading the way, Chris will discover that everything that seems to be occurring on the space station is merely a projection of the unhealed thoughts in his own mind.

Introduction

If you were on a desert island and could request one movie, this would be the one to ask for! *Solaris* is a beautiful illustration of True Forgiveness; it is literally a life raft out of this world. Several lines of the Dylan Thomas poem "Death Shall Have No Dominion" are heard in the movie and capsulize it beautifully:

Though they go mad they shall be sane,
Though they sink through the sea they shall rise again;
Though lovers be lost love shall not;
And death shall have no dominion.

The planet Solaris is the representation of abstract Love, Light, and Oneness. One of the most well-known passages in the Course states, "The course does not aim at teaching the meaning of love, for that is beyond what can be taught. It does aim, however, at removing the blocks to the awareness of love's presence, which is your natural inheritance." In-1 Since Oneness is realized by looking at and releasing false ego beliefs, Solaris reflects whatever issues are unresolved and unforgiven in the unconscious mind. It pushes up all of the darkness—the blocks to Love's awareness—so that they may be healed.

Through numerous flashbacks in the movie, we discover that Chris used to be married to a woman named Rheya. The flashbacks show Chris and Rheya's meeting and courtship, with hints as to her disturbed upbringing and emotional difficulties. They also reveal that Rheya once terminated a pregnancy but did not tell Chris about it. When he finds out he is distraught and walks out on her. Rheya then commits suicide and is later found by Chris when he returns home. The pain associated with Rheya's suicide is still buried in Chris' mind. He feels a huge sense of loss, regret, guilt, and inadequacy. He feels like he failed Rheya, and lost his last chance to make things right when she committed suicide.

Solaris is going to give Chris a chance to set it straight! Let's imagine going to Solaris. What are the unresolved thoughts and issues that are still revolving around in our mind? Because those unhealed areas are what would manifest immediately; there wouldn't be a delay where the experience would seem to spread out over linear time. The cause of unrest in the mind would be immediately present, it would be right in front of us to be released.

We can think of it this way: If someone gave us a hot potato to hold, we would drop it pretty quickly because the effect would seem to be immediate and direct. When an upsetting issue is projected out over time, however, it seems to be a long and lengthy process because we believe that cause and effect are apart.

Solaris is teaching us that cause and effect are together. If we release the false cause in our mind, we also release all the effects—pain, suffering, and upset—that seemed to be a result of that cause. That is what True Forgiveness really is. When we truly forgive the belief that we could have ever existed outside of the Mind of God, Innocence reigns! We realize that we have never done anything wrong, and everything is forgiven because it never happened in Reality!

Whenever we have a sense of hurt, pain, grief, loss—or any feeling other than joy—it is because we are holding an egoic thought in our mind. Our feelings may seem to stem from an event that happened in the past, or to be a concern about something that may happen in the future, but that isn't the case; they come from a present fear. To believe otherwise is just an attempt to cover over the present moment, the holy instant, with a false idea. The good news is that a present release is possible. It's not a matter of time; we have the power to release our mind from pain, suffering, and illusions *now*. We tend to believe that forgiveness may take many lifetimes of inner work and processing, that it is a huge thought reversal, but it actually requires only the tiniest little tweak in perspective.

Solaris is the ultimate forgiveness movie. It is not forgiveness the way the world teaches it, which is to believe that someone has done us wrong and we have to find a way to bless them. With True Forgiveness, we start to realize that we were mistaken about everything we have ever perceived. This opens the gateway to healing, the gateway to true freedom. Even thinking we were only ninety-nine percent wrong would not do it, because even a one-percent inkling that we might be right would prevent our full awareness from opening to this healing power.

David's Movie Commentary

Scene: *Chris, before leaving earth, accidentally cuts his finger while chopping vegetables. As he rinses it in the sink, he looks at the cut.*

Take note of this scene. It is a crucial scene that repeats at the end of the movie with a deep teaching.

Scene: *Once aboard the space station, Chris finds Snow, one of the two surviving crew members and asks him what is happening on the ship. Snow replies, "I could tell you what's happening, but I don't know if it would really tell you what's happening."*

There is no way for Snow to explain what is happening to Chris because Chris is thinking in linear terms, and linearity is the block to the awareness of forgiveness. It is impossible to understand forgiveness from the linear way of looking at things. We have to give up everything we think in linear terms to experience where this movie is taking us. Here are some interesting things to notice. First, our main character is named Chris, which is one letter short of Christ. Then there are the lyrics to the song that was playing as Chris first walked down the corridor of the space station: "Prepare to go down into the riddle, the riddle, the riddle." We have to go down into the riddle of the ego in order to transcend it. While Chris and Snow are talking, the lyric in the background is, "The joke's on you. The joke's on you." This whole ego world, this whole time-space continuum and all of linearity, is playing the biggest joke on us. It is playing a huge game of hide and seek. We have forgotten our Christ identity and gotten caught up into a personality self.

Going into the riddle of our mind, all the way towards enlightenment, means we have to empty the mind of everything we think we think and think we know. Buddha called this state of emptiness the "void." Beyond the seeming void is the Kingdom of Heaven, which is Everything. It is the Everything-ness of Who we are.

Chris is taking his first steps into the riddle of the mind. He is trying to use his skills as a psychologist to understand the situation on board the ship. When the answer to his question, "Can you tell me what is happening up here?" is "I could tell you what's happening, but that wouldn't really tell you what is happening," he is perplexed. Likewise, the Course is perplexing for many because it dismantles every aspect of linear thinking. Those who try to maintain the linear perspective—that is, the story of their lives, their self-concept—will resist learning the Course because it leaves only the Present Moment, which is the gateway to Eternity.

Scene: Chris is getting ready to go to sleep in his room on board the space station.

Freud called dreams "wish fulfillment." Everything we are dreaming in our unconscious mind, during what we call night-time sleep, is just our belief system being acted out. We can say the same thing regarding what we call our daily life. Down to the tiniest little detail, it is all fantasy and wish fulfillment; it is nothing more than a collection of images and scenarios made up by the ego. Although in this scene Chris appears to be drifting into sleep, nothing is unconscious on Solaris. Everything is acted out.

Scene: Chris wakes up in the morning in response to a caress from his wife, Rheya, who committed suicide several years ago. When he sees her, he jumps out of bed and runs across the room to get away from her.

Chris is terrified and disbelieving when he sees Rheya; he is psychologically shattered. Her appearance brings into question every concept he has about death. On earth, in linear time, when someone dies, there is a sense of them being out of awareness. Chris can't accept the possibility that Rheya is real because it doesn't fit into his belief system. He is so frightened that he wants only to get away from her.

At the end of the scene, Chris, who is still frightened by Rheya, tells her he needs to leave and check on the crew. Rheya screams, "No, no, don't leave me, don't leave me." Her reaction seems to indicate that she is afraid of loss and separation, but when Chris asks her why she doesn't want him to leave, she looks confused and says she doesn't know. What is really going on is that Rheya is acting out *Chris'* fear of being left. He believes that when she committed suicide, he lost her from his life, and this fear of abandonment is still an unhealed thought in his mind.

Scene: *Chris locks Rheya in an escape pod and ejects her off into space.*

This is quite a breakup scene! Chris is so frightened by Rheya seeming to manifest that he actually sends her into space! This is an example of projection. When there is a grievance in our mind that we cannot deal with, we try to get rid of it. Grievances are the past repeated over and over again. It is the same old script of personal, private minds and private thoughts. As long as this perspective of separate people remains, the grievances repeat continuously. By sending her into space, Chris reenacts the deep grievance he has with Rheya due to her committing suicide after an argument between them.

Scene: *The next night, Chris dreams about Rheya and in the morning she is in bed with him once again. Chris asks her what she remembers and all she knows is her life with him on earth; she has no memory of how she arrived at the space station. When Rheya asks Chris, "So I wasn't here yesterday?" He replies, "No."*

Already the lies are starting. Part of the problem with this kind of interaction is that it lacks consistency. When we seem to lie to somebody, we are really lying to ourselves, because there is only One Mind. When we believe we have to say something untruthful in order to protect someone or avoid hurting their feelings, it is an indication of underlying fear. Chris is people-pleasing in order to avoid telling Rheya that she *was* there the day before, but that he had ejected her into space.

This represents a conflict inside the mind. Jesus says in the Course that we first look inside, and then we look outside and seem to see a world. But the world simply acts out the conflict in the ego mind. Much of it is unconscious, pushed out of awareness, but what we see outside is a pictorial, motion-picture representation of what we are feeling and believing in our minds. When we recognize this, we think, "I am going to start paying much more attention to my mind. I'm going to stop feeling guilty about things in the world, because they are really not the cause at all."

The Holy Spirit uses what the ego made. Take the book *A Course in Miracles*, for example. The Holy Spirit is using the words that the ego invented in a way that points back to the Holy Spirit. But since the Course itself is part of the past, the ego had to have made the Course—it projected out the whole cosmos. This character, David, was part of the projection. Jesus was part of the projection. Buddha, Krishna, and Mother Theresa were part of the projection as well and the Holy Spirit can use all of these symbols. Seeing it this way reminds the mind that it made it all up.

The Holy Spirit is calling forth witnesses in a miraculous way. He uses the same symbols that were used for hate, pain, shame, and guilt, to take us through the escape hatch in our own mind. Through forgiveness, we escape the world and return to the One Mind, to God.

Scene: *While having a conversation with Snow, Chris flashes back to the fight he and Rheya had just before she committed suicide. At the same time, Rheya, looking out at Solaris, seems to remember bits and pieces of the scene as well. Later, when Chris and Rheya are speaking, she tells him that she is not the person she remembers.*

Rheya has begun to have doubts about who she really is. She has all the memories of her life with Chris, but they feel like they don't belong to her. She tells Chris that she doesn't understand what is happening and that she doesn't think she can live this way. Let's look again at these lines in the Dylan Thomas poem:

Though lovers be lost love shall not,
And death shall have no dominion.

In *Solaris*, the appearance of love between husband and wife shall seem to be lost, to disappear in linear time, but the Divine Love of the

Spirit shall not. The cosmos was made as a veil to cover over Divine Love. Nothing in this world can approximate that Divine Love except enlightenment, or the happy dream.

In the happy dream, miracles seem to happen on a daily basis, and we experience a deep love that is not dependent on appearances such as bodies being together. The New Testament of the Bible says that the things of time, the temporal, shall pass away, and the eternal will last forever. That is the teaching of *A Course in Miracles* as well. In this world, "love" is projected out and associated with images, and we often experience heartbreak when they seem to change. But these images of love that involve bodies and forms are temporary. Even the husband-wife construct that seems to be love in this world will pass away. Only Love, eternal life, goes on forever. That is our true Identity, which remains in God.

The poem "And Death Shall Have No Dominion" is a call into eternal life. *Solaris* shows us that everything is experienced in the mind. When we change our mind, we change the way we look at the world—and that is how we get back to eternal life.

Scene: *Chris awakes in the night to find his friend Gibarian, who committed suicide before Chris arrived, standing in his room. Chris asks, "What does Solaris want from us?" and Gibarian responds "Why do you think it has to want something? This is why you have to leave. If you keep thinking there's a solution, you'll die here."*

There are no solutions. We see how applicable that is to our work with *A Course in Miracles*. When we try to figure out anything about this world, we will die here, because there is no solution to be found in the projection of time and space. We will never find the answer in form. Sometimes people find the Course and think it will give them all the answers. But even the Course is just a symbol; it's a ladder that is helping us to go inside our mind. The only way to find the answer is to *experience* the answer after we have questioned all the false beliefs. The book can't do it for us. The book is just a reflection of our mind's desire to wake up and forgive.

Although Chris came to the space station for the sole purpose of trying to figure out what was happening, now he is being presented with the idea that he *can't* figure it out. Chris' question, "What does it want from us?" is interesting. The answer is, "Why do you think it has to want something from you?"

Gibarian is basically telling Chris that Solaris does not want anything from them, just as the Holy Spirit does not want anything from us. The Holy Spirit wants to offer us a gift, which is a correction, a solution to the whole dream. The Holy Spirit is the answer, and as long as we look for it in form, we do not want to hear the real answer. We want to hear a pseudo, make-believe answer of the world, but that never settles anything. We may think we have found an answer—that there are people or a theology or a belief system we can trust. But in the end even that will wash away, because there is no answer to be found in form. No matter how many decisions or choices we make in the world, we will not find an answer in form.

Scene: Gibarian says to Chris, "Do you understand what I'm trying to tell you? There are no answers, only choices."

Gibarian's words indicate that there is a choice to make. As we know from the Course, there is a choice in the mind. The choice is very simple. Which voice am I going to listen to: the ego or the Holy Spirit? The ego makes it seem very complex by teaching us that there are choices in the world, and we should put effort and energy into making the right ones. But our mind training is showing us that we have to align with God and be with the Holy Spirit. Choosing the Holy Spirit consistently is how we escape from the dream of the world and find the happy dream. Many of the dialogues throughout the movie are very helpful because they point to practical application of the teachings.

Scene: Dr. Gordon and Chris get into an argument after she tells Rheya that Chris ejected her into space the first time she manifested. Dr. Gordon tells Chris that he is being manipulated. She says, "If she was ugly, you wouldn't want her around. That's why she's not ugly. She's a mirror that reflects part of your mind and you provide the form. She's a copy, a facsimile."

We could say that all people are facsimiles. They look and act and seem real; they seem to have lives and minds of their own. They seem to have their own thoughts, actions, emotions, and memories. It seems as though they really exist. But people are not whole; they are like holograms. We don't think of people as holograms. We think, "Mom! Dad!" But human beings, like the rest of the entire cosmos, are a projection of the ego mind. Since the ego mind sees only the past, all of its images are fragmented and partial; they are not whole and complete. Jesus describes this in Workbook Lesson two of the Course: "I have given everything I see all the meaning it has for me." W-2

Chris is upset and angry because he sees Rheya as a real person. But what is a real person? There is no such thing. We are speaking to images! It is like talking to puppets that are acting out exactly what our ego mind told them to do and say. We gave them the parts; we have given the characters all the meaning they seem to have. Everything is acted out exactly as we want it to be. It is fantasy. It is wish fulfillment. And it is all exactly according to the instructions that were given.

If we think that others are separate from us, have a will apart from ours, and are doing something to us that we don't like, we must ask ourselves how they got out there in the first place. The answer is that they are not out there—they are grievances, judgments, and partial memories that have been projected by our mind onto the screen and are now seen as real people.

This is what happens in the fairy tale Pinocchio. There is Geppetto, the puppet maker, Jiminy Cricket who plays the conscience, and Pinocchio, a wooden puppet that wanted to become a real boy, an autonomous boy, not just a puppet on a string. He wanted to have a mind of his own, desires of his own, and a life of his own. And then he got his wish. He became a real boy who was independent and could think for himself. And as soon as he could, he didn't want Jiminy Cricket around anymore. He didn't want that conscience speaking to him and guiding him. Pinocchio said, "I am not listening to you anymore," and he went off to Pleasure Island. A bizarre thing happened to him there—he got turned into a donkey! All from trying to have an autonomous will and be a "real boy."

Once we realize that none of the images are real, then we experience that the body we thought was our own and the bodies we thought belonged to others, are simply instruments that the Holy Spirit can use. In a sense, we get back on the strings, and we let the Holy Spirit move the crossbar. We literally let the Holy Spirit speak through us, act through us—do everything through us—instead of trying to play the part of an autonomous individual.

Scene: *Chris wakes up in the middle of the night, and Rheya is not there. He goes and looks for her and discovers that she has attempted suicide by drinking liquid oxygen. Although her face is burned and she appears to be dead, Rheya comes back to life as Chris watches. When she wakes up and Chris says her name, she responds "Don't call me that," and pushes him away. Later, Rheya says to Chris, "Don't you see? I came from your memory of her. That's the problem. I'm not a whole person. In your memory, you get to control everything, so even if you remember something wrong, I am predetermined to carry it out. I'm suicidal because that's how you remember me. My voice sounds the way it does because that's how you remember it." When she asks Chris, "But am I really Rheya? He responds, "I don't know anymore. All I see is you."*

Chris doesn't care that Rheya might not be a real person; he wants to hold onto the husband-wife image, which he sees as part of his self-concept. He believes this concept is what love is, and he doesn't want to lose it. When we hold on to a fabrication of a life that is not a real life, we are making a bargain with the ego. Nothing of the cosmos seemed to arrive until there was an agreement to believe in the ego. Rheya, who understands this, is telling him he has to let it go, to surrender because it isn't real.

Scene: *As Rheya gazes out of the space station window at Solaris, she tells Chris, "You and I must have an arrangement, some kind of unspoken understanding, that I am not really a human being." She adds, "We could never have a life together. It would be impossible."*

In the Course, Jesus speaks of this unspoken agreement as the cornerstone of the ego thought system. We are afraid to lift this cornerstone because the ego has told us that we did separate from God, that God is angry with us, and that we will be punished. It says that if we lift the cornerstone of this bargain that was signed in blood, God will strike us dead.

The Holy Spirit, however, says, *No, let's go back to the original error. You will see that none of it is real, that none of it ever happened. We will lift this false belief together; we will raise it to the light and I'll show you that God loves you, and that you could never separate from Him.* The reason why it gets so intense when we go deeper and deeper into our mind is that the ego is using everything it's got to stop us from discovering this.

Scene: Rheya knows Dr. Gordon has developed an apparatus that can permanently destroy a "visitor" and Rheya wants Chris to let Dr. Gordon use the device on her. Driven by his own grief and guilt over the "real" Rheya's suicide, Chris begins ingesting a chemical stimulant so he can stay awake and prevent Rheya from leaving their room at night.

This is Chris' desperate attempt to avoid repeating the past and essentially abandoning Rheya to suicide. When his mind projected Rheya the first time, Chris was so frightened that he wanted her gone right away, and sent her off in a pod. But now his fear is that she will leave. Chris is feeling attachment and attraction to Rheya, and he doesn't want to lose her. We can see how trying to get rid of her and trying to hold onto her both cause enormous strain. They are the same dilemma; each is an attempt to manage the guilt he feels over her death.

In spite of his extreme efforts, one night Chris finally falls asleep and dreams about finding Rheya after her suicide. She was clutching the Dylan Thomas poem in her hand as a suicide note. Chris still blames himself for her death.

When he wakes up, he finds that Rheya has left the room and convinced Dr. Gordon to destroy her with the apparatus. She has left a goodbye video message for Chris in which she tells him that she went through his things and found the suicide note that he brought with him from earth. It made her realize that she is not Rheya. She says she knows he loved her and that she loved him too, and wishes they could live inside that feeling forever. She finishes by saying that maybe there's a place where they can, but she knows it's not on earth and it's not on the ship.

Scene: In a rage, Chris confronts Dr. Gordon about using the device on Rheya. She defends what she did and told him that Rheya begged her to do it. Dr. Gordon says that she has decided to return to earth, she is going home. As she turns the space station's operating systems back on, Chris notices blood on the ceiling tiles, and they discover the real Snow stuffed in the ceiling, dead. Chris and Dr. Gordon go and confront Snow, who admits that he is a "visitor" and that it is his brother who is dead. He says that he killed him in self-defense when his brother attacked him. He suggests that Chris and Dr. Gordon lock him in his room and return to earth. They do so, and prepare to leave. Dr. Gordon precedes Chris into the escape pod, and Chris pauses as though undecided.

Chris is at a major choice point—he can either join Dr. Gordon in the escape pod and go back to earth, or he can turn and face the Light that he's been so afraid to look at.

Scene: Chris is riding in a train on earth. In a voiceover, he says, "Earth. Even the word sounded strange to me now... unfamiliar. How long had I been gone? How long had I been back? Did it matter? I tried to find the rhythm of the world where I used to live. I followed the current. I was silent, attentive, I made a conscious effort to smile, nod, stand, and perform the millions of gestures that constitute life on earth. I studied these gestures until they became reflexes again. But I was haunted by the idea that I remembered her wrong, and somehow I was wrong about everything."

"Haunted by the idea that I remembered her wrong"—that is the key! Chris sees that he remembers Rheya only from the past, from a partial memory, and he finally realizes that is the problem. We all have to come to this point of realization. When we think about anybody that we've had a grievance with in our life, anyone who has seemingly harmed us in some way or taken advantage of us, we can open our mind to the realization that we are remembering them wrong. The form of the memory doesn't matter because they are all only partial memories.

Admitting that we have a perceptual problem—"I have remembered everything wrong"—is the gateway to true healing. Without this, we will continue to think that we are right about what we have perceived, right about what we think has happened. When we would rather be right than happy, we are stuck. The only way we can experience happiness is to admit that we have remembered it wrong. Whatever the scenario, person, place, or circumstance was, we remember it wrong.

Scene: Chris accidentally cuts his finger while chopping vegetables. As he rinses it in the sink, he looks at the cut, which immediately heals. Chris turns and gazes at a photo of Rheya.

This is the scene that was shown earlier in the movie, with one key difference. This time when Chris cuts his finger, it heals right away. This healing is symbolic of the forgiveness that has taken place in Chris' mind.

Scene: The movie returns to the scene where Chris is in the space station watching Dr. Gordon enter the escape pod ahead of him. He looks at Solaris and makes his decision. Chris closes the hatch on the escape pod behind Dr. Gordon and turns the other way.

Chris has made his decision. He wants the light of Solaris, which represents the Light in our mind. Every time we get caught up in roles, distractions, busy doings, comparisons, judgments, and so on, we are falling for the ego's tricks; we are avoiding going into the Light. That is why Jesus says that the dreams we think we like can hold us back as much as those in which the fear is seen.

It is essential to watch our mind and see where we are attracted to anything in the ego's thought system, which is like quicksand. When we are attracted to something of the world, it is actually a delay maneuver to prevent us from getting to the escape hatch and waking up. This is why we have to become more and more tuned into Spirit, more and more willing to be a vehicle for the expression of Spirit.

We need to let Spirit use our body, our resources—anything we seem to have in the dream world. We don't have anything anyway because we can't really own anything. The dream world is just images. If we think we own or possess anything in the world, then we believe that to own nothing is to own something. When we start to get more aligned with Spirit, we realize that the only way to find peace, joy, and happiness is to start to see that nothing is nothing, and follow our heart instead. The ego says that this will be a sacrifice. But it is not a sacrifice to let go of our attachments and wake up to eternal life.

Workbook Lesson 128 says, "The world I see holds nothing that I want." Once we get into that vibe, the Holy Spirit can give the world back to us in a whole new way, as the happy dream, or the real world. But as long as we still want something from the world, we are letting the ego hold a world of fragmented perception in place. When we get to the point where we don't want anything from anybody, or anything from the world, we realize that it never had anything to offer. When we say, "That's it! I'm through. I'm finished. It's over!" and we mean it, then the Holy Spirit will give it back to us, cleansed of the ego's purpose. Then we will see a beautiful, happy, whole world before it disappears and we wake up to Heaven.

The Course poses this question: "Do I want to see what I denied *because* it is the truth?" T-21.VII.5 That is to say, "Do I want to see the Light because it is the truth?" There is no going back after we answer yes to that.

Scene: *Snow smiles joyfully as he realizes his total innocence in the light. As the space station falls into the light of Solaris, Chris crumples to the floor, seemingly dying. Gibarian's son appears and looks calmly down at him. The child extends his hand, and slowly Chris reaches up and takes it.*

Chris has chosen enlightenment—True Forgiveness—and is now walking directly into the Light of Christ. He is going back to God. This feels very intense to the ego, which knows that moving into the Light completely means letting go completely of the self-concept, of our belief in individuality. There is no individuality in Oneness, and this is extremely threatening to the ego, which relies on the belief in separation in order to survive.

The fear of death is the fear of losing existence, and so the ego sees going towards the Light as death. Chris' crumpling to the floor is symbolic of the fear of dying. When the little boy appears with his hand outstretched, it is a calm symbol of invitation: Come with me. Taking the boy's hand is symbolic of rising up. That is the true resurrection—not the resurrection of the body, but the resurrection of the mind. The Bible says that a little child shall lead the way. Here is the child of innocence saying with his eyes, *Welcome home.* Surrendering to Oneness is our only option. It is only when we become willing to let go of our self-concept and yield to the Light that an experience of True Love can come in to take the place of fear.

Scene: Chris is once again back on earth in his kitchen, looking at the photo of Rheya, and this time he hears her speak his name. When he turns around, Rheya is standing there smiling at him. Chris asks, "Am I alive or dead?" and Rheya smiles and replies, "We don't have to think like that anymore. We're together now. Everything we've done is forgiven, everything." They embrace, and the scene dissolves into the light of Solaris.

It doesn't get any clearer than that! That's the whole step. The last scene is a perfect reflection of "as above, so below." It shows what has occurred in the mind, which is a merging back with the Light, an accepting of the Atonement. It is a beautiful expression of the happy dream, where everything is forgiven. Duality is gone! "Here" or "there" is gone. Earth, time, and space are gone. We don't need to think like that anymore. Even the question of being alive or dead, which seems like such a big question on earth, is irrelevant in the end.

Am I physically alive or dead? Am I psychologically alive or dead? We don't need to think like that anymore. Am I married or not? Am I with him or not? We don't need to think like that anymore. These thoughts of duality are where the conflict is. And the forgiveness, the experience of unification of the mind, is where the healing is.

All of these questions are essentially the same, and actually they are not even true questions—they are statements. Questions such as do I want this thing or that thing, do I want to be here or there, are all saying the same thing: I'm an ego; how can I make the best of it with this terrible situation of being fallen from grace? That's not really a question at all. It reinforces the illusion.

To begin waking up, we must ask a True question, such as, "Do I want to wake up and know my Creator?" The answer to that question brings a completely different experience. Another True question is, "Do I want to see this world differently?" This is a higher-order question, which leads to a totally different way of looking at the world.

Awakening is a matter of coming to that purification of desire where we want only one thing. Jesus says that when we want only love, we will look upon nothing else; we will see only love. Our mind then becomes so unified that the world disappears. Thank You God, for the glimpse of how simple it can be. Everything is forgiven, everything! Wow, that's a statement of pure innocence!

Chapter 7

TIME AND QUANTUM

Living based on the belief in linear time is absurd. Time is just a construct. The world of linear time can't be changed, so there is no point in trying to. We need to change our mind instead.

A Course in Miracles says that the script is written. "Written" is past tense; it is the sense of being over. "The script is written" emphasizes that time is the past. It is saying that time is over and that we can't change it. Once we begin to grasp that in full awareness, we cease to play the game of trying to fix it.

The ego, however, teaches that time is not over, and that the world, people, and personalities *can* be changed. It puts a strong emphasis on changing the form. It has to be one or the other. We can't be the Holy Christ—Everything there is—and be limited by a cosmos of illusion that seems to be occupying some time-space coordinates. It has to be one or the other. Are we the quantum field or are we a specific outcome of belief?

As we look at time and "the script is written" from the perspective of Spirit, we can feel our mind start to expand. We start to think that maybe we're not so limited after all, that maybe we are vastness and wholeness. When we consistently look through Spirit's perspective, we can get into the joy of being; we can actually lose track of the passage of time. That's the fun of this awakening experience.

The Spirit deals with what we believe and what we perceive, and this is highly practical. As the Spirit works with us in this way, we find ourselves becoming detached from and dis-identified with the world. We are not disoriented anymore; we feel no sense of confusion. We are Everything that is, and in that realization there is a sense of glory. If somebody asks us how we're doing, we can reply, "I'm all there is." That's the feeling. There's a majesty to it, a vastness. The Spirit *is* that vastness.

Chapter 8

EMISSARY

Note

The mini-movie *Time's End* is an edited version of *Star Trek: Deep Space Nine*: Season 1, Episode 1, Parts 1 and 2: "Emissary," 1993. The mini-movie is available for viewing at the online *Movie Watcher's Guide to Enlightenment*.

Key Themes

- Taking Responsibility for State of Mind
- Linear Time

Movie Synopsis

Commander Benjamin Sisko is assigned by Starfleet as station commander of "Deep Space Nine," which is in orbit of Bajor, with the purpose of helping Bajor enter into the Federation. Sisko is traveling to the station aboard the Enterprise, which is led by Captain Picard. In an earlier episode, Captain Picard, while under Borg control, ordered an attack on Sisko's Starfleet ship. Sisko's wife Jennifer was killed during the attack. Sisko is resentful of this current duty, holding Captain Picard responsible. When the Enterprise arrives at the station, Sisko informs Captain Picard that he is contemplating resigning from Starfleet to seek a civilian position, but that he will continue as ordered to perform his job as station commander, until Captain Picard finds a replacement.

Introduction

Grievances go beyond the person, beyond the specific personal memory. We have a memory problem: the mind recalls the past; it wants something of the past, of time and space, to be real. As long as it wants something in time and space to be real, it calls forth scenarios.

The mind relentlessly continues bringing up the past. It does this until we have a breakthrough in which we realize that all the memories are the same, the good memories *and* the bad. The ego tries to deny and repress the negative ones, and to hold on to and keep the positive ones. Only when everything is finally integrated and it is seen that they are all the same, do we have a real breakthrough, a true healing.

In "Emissary", we have the initial context of a relationship with an embedded grievance that gets deeper and deeper. Sisko's assignment is to help the Bajorians recover from an occupation. They are spiritually advanced and possess a glowing green orb that has the power to show scenes from the past. The light, in the movie portrayed in human light form, calls forth these scenes in mind, so that they can be seen as unreal and invalid.

"Emissary" is a masterpiece, and cannot be watched often enough. It gives a new awareness of how the mind uses memory, and helps in letting all prior understanding go. We can apply this new awareness to any memory or grievance we have and experience a total transformation. It is essential to realize that positive and negative memories are the same. This movie shows that all repressed memories have to be brought up to the light and seen for the nothingness that they are.

David's Movie Commentary

Scene: *When Sisko visits the spiritual leader Kai Opaka on Bajor, she shows him a glowing green orb. It is one of nine such orbs that have appeared in the sky over 10,000 years and his task is to retrieve the missing orbs from the Temple. She explains that his mission has nothing to do with the form of returning the orbs; the journey is for reclaiming his own power. She tells him, "I cannot give you what you will not give yourself. Look for solutions from within."*

This is a powerful scene because we see how Sisko represents the "I know" mind. He knows his technology, but he does not realize that it blocks him from going into his mind and knowing the reality within. All he has is his "I know mind" and his anger and rage, which are tied into guilt.

The Bajorian orb has the power to give deep insights into truth. Opaka reads his mind right away and sees how ironic it is that Sisko has been sent as the messenger to help them when he is spiritually shallow and doesn't even want to be there. Sisko does not have a clue that it is *he* who is going to have a major transformation. He is about to undergo a huge dismantling of all that he thinks he knows about everything, including time and space. The orb is going to give him glimpses that will bring about this dismantling.

Scene: *Sisko and his colleague Dax take a spacecraft to investigate the Denorios Belt. They enter a wormhole and land somewhere "unknown." Upon stepping out onto the landscape, Commander Sisko sees a stormy and blackened landscape and Officer Dax sees a sunny, peaceful garden.*

The first Workbook Lesson in *A Course in Miracles* is, "Nothing I see means anything." W-1 This means that no two people see the same world. None of the seven billion people on the planet see the same world. Looking through the ego's lens, everyone sees a different world, because the ego lens is one of fragmentation. In Truth, there are not multiple people. The belief that there could be private minds with private thoughts is all part of the distortion. And that is why relationships are so difficult.

Scene: *The green orb appears and seems to "shoot" at Sisko. He is thrown to the ground and Officer Dax disappears completely. She reappears moments later on board the Deep Space Nine Station, while Sisko finds himself going into the Light. Once inside the Light, Sisko sees images of his wife, friends, and crew members appear before him. As he begins to explain who he is and what life as a human being consists of, the Light beings ask him deep and probing questions. They cannot conceive of the concepts he is sharing. They ask questions such as: What is "time?" What is "experience?" What is "lost?" When Sisko talks about the concept of "loss" they say, "It is inconceivable that any species could exist in such a manner!"*

As humans, when we sit down and start talking to somebody, we tell our story, the other person tells their story, and we call this exchange of stories an encounter. Just as the world seems to be solid, stories seem to be very linear and concrete—filled with grievances, victimization, and loss. But there is a deeper Presence within us that can use the stories to point us in the right direction. When we listen to that Presence, it begins to dawn on us that perhaps we don't need to be telling those stories any longer because they are all starting to sound the same. We can go and sit peacefully under a tree instead.

To the Light, a linear existence is absolutely inconceivable. In this movie, we will see the contrast between linear time and simultaneity. Once we forgive the idea of linear time, we will lose every care that we have ever had. It will become impossible to hold a grievance. The ego will not have a chance in our mind. Game over.

Scene: *Sisko is telling the Light that the "value" of linear time is that what is going to happen is unknown. Using the analogy of baseball, he shares that "the game wouldn't be worth playing if we knew what would happen." He shares that the unknown defines human existence. The Light asks, "So you value your ignorance of what is to come?"*

The ego values the idea of potentiality because we allow it to distract us. We seek to become better; we strive to achieve things in the world, such as a family and a career. It is the potential of wanting something and enjoying the excitement of thinking, *I can make anything of my life that I want. I have huge potential.* But all of that is based on linearity. There is no potential in linear time. We only have the opportunity to wake up to our eternal nature, which is abstract love and light.

The movie makes it clear that there is nothing fascinating about this world. The sooner we can begin to see this, the sooner we will be ready for a spectacular experience that will knock our socks off. It will blow our mind more than any drug we could take. It is a permanent fix for our mind, because it shows us that the world contains nothing. Jesus sums it up, "The world I see holds nothing that I want." W-128

When Jesus taught, "The Father and I are One," he was saying that there is only one Spirit. There is not a Father and a Son, only pure, complete, total, absolute Oneness. The problem occurs due to our crazy belief in the separation of cause and effect. That belief generates a whole cosmos of time and space, and all the hypotheticals that come with it.

Thoughts about what our life can be in the future or what we are going to do tomorrow are hypotheticals. The entire cosmos consists of hypothetical scenarios, and none of them have any meaning. There are not some that are to come or some that have already happened— all of them are simultaneous. As long as we hold onto the linear perspective, we will continue to experience grievances, suffering, and loss. They are inevitable when we take the linear perspective.

This movie shows that the Light does not comprehend linearity. The Light is asking, "You value your ignorance of what is to come?" When we are excited about potentials in the future, we are valuing ignorance; we are playing a game of hide and seek with our True Self. To do this is to pretend that we do not know who we really are. We can get lost in this pretense, forgetting the Presence of what is real and true.

Scene: As Sisko attempts to explain his human existence to the Light, he repeatedly appears back at the scene where his wife died. Finally he asks, "What is the point of bringing me back to this?" "You exist here," says the Light, "you bring us here." Sisko implores them, "Then give me the power to lead you somewhere else, anywhere else!" The Light responds, "We cannot give you what you deny yourself. Look for solutions from within! You choose to live here. It is not linear; you exist here!"

The Light is helping Sisko to be aware of his decision for the wrong mind. *A Course in Miracles* says that the key to healing is choosing between the right mind and the wrong mind. "Heaven is the decision I must make." W-138 Hell is a wrong-minded decision; however, in Truth even it has no real effect. Nothing has ever happened to us in linear time—no pain, hurt, or grievances that could upset us, nor anything that could bring us happiness. The decision for Heaven is purely in the mind, in consciousness.

Before he got to Bajor, Sisko wanted to exist in the memories of pleasure—the good memories. He wanted to run away and hide from the memories of hurt and pain. He was avoiding the memory of being on a burning ship and seeing his wife die because it triggered such intense hurt and pain. He had a deep sense of loss associated with that memory.

When the Light tells Sisko that he is the one bringing them back to the scene of his wife's death over and over, they are telling him that he is choosing to *live* in this past memory instead of seeing that he merely exists there. We exist everywhere. We do not exist in some memories, and not in others. We exist in all the memories. All the memories are together in an integrated mind, in the whole mind.

The experience of the happy dream, or the real world, is the experience of unified perception, or the quantum field. Once we've had this realization, we see that we have existed in all memories, across all time. We have seemed to exist in both the good and bad memories, and yet the experience of the happy dream is when we are not identified with any of the memories as who we are. We have transcended them all. We exist in the Light. It is beautiful.

The Light is calling Sisko to integrate his mind, to start to see that everything is simultaneous, everything is Oneness, everything is Light. All our pain comes from believing in and dividing up our memories and experiences and saying, "I exist in this one but not the other. I like this one but not that one. I am attracted to the pleasure, but I am going to avoid the pain."

We learn from *A Course in Miracles* that it is impossible to seek for pleasure without finding pain. The ego does not want this idea brought into awareness because when we start to realize that pleasure and pain are identical—and that is the trap of this world—then we are ready for a miracle that takes us beyond time and space. The ego wants us to keep pursuing pleasure and avoiding pain, and that is what Sisko has been doing with his linear life. That is the whole purpose of linearity.

The benefit of an integrated mind is that we feel an immense gratitude and appreciation for everyone and everything as we see that all of our grievances were merely misperceptions. Sisko is now ready for a total reinterpretation of his "enemy," Captain Picard. Look at the potential this has! It is a good glimpse of what the spiritual journey is about.

There is no right or wrong, good or bad. It is irrelevant when we watch a movie with commentary like this whether we are elated or totally repulsed. The commentary is a non-compromising message, and this is what the spiritual journey is authentically about—being convinced of our reality in eternity. And to do that, we have to see the *unreality* of linear time.

The Holy Spirit has to convince us that reality is better than illusions and that eternity is better than linear time. It is actually beyond one being better than the other; it is a case of there being no comparison. One is real and one is not. If we are sincerely interested in experiencing True Happiness, if we really want to be in a miraculous state of mind, all it takes is the willingness to start to see the miracle offers us everything.

When we are being trained to be a miracle worker, to be aligned with our Source, we light up in the joy of Heaven. We see that this alignment offers us everything and that the world, with all of its beliefs in linearity and concepts, offers absolutely nothing. We open to a life of joy in which we have no fear of consequences.

If we start to see the reality of the Light, and the unreality of the world, what concerns could we have about jobs, about family, about country? What concerns could we have about physical well-being or beauty? What does beauty mean in the context of the Light? What do skills and abilities and intelligence mean? When we start to realize that intelligence, ambition, and success—as the world defines them—are a joke, we can easily let them go. When we look at all the "isms:" capitalism, socialism, sexism, racism, even mysticism, we can give them all up. Why? Because words are not Awareness. Words are like little springboards and pointers. They can be used by Spirit in a beautiful, graceful way, but we will never reach an actual experience through words.

We have to go deeply into our consciousness to discover the impossibility of hurt, the impossibility of pain, the impossibility of sickness.

These things are impossible because God did not create them. Love does not create hurt. Love does not create pain. Love does not create suffering. As we give our mistaken beliefs over; we say, "Thank you!" It is a revelatory moment indeed! From then on there's no *A Course in Miracles*, no pathway. There is only an experience of transcendence. That is what a miracle does. It shows us our reality, and the impossibility of anything other than our reality.

Our task as miracle workers is to face our fearful thoughts head on, to let them come up and embrace them. This includes all of our private thoughts, even the ones we feel are insignificant. The Light can handle them. It is not shaking before them. When we stop hiding and protecting our fearful thoughts, the Truth of Who We Are begins to shine in our mind. If somebody asks us how we are doing, we can say, "I am the quantum field." Or we can try this one out: "I am the goal the world is searching for." W-318

Scene: Sisko is thrust back through the wormhole in his small spacecraft and returns to the station. Captain Picard arrives at the station aboard the Enterprise. Having faced his belief in loss, and seeing that he was only hurting himself, Sisko tells Captain Picard that he would like to stay on as commander of the station; he then reaches out to shake his hand. Sisko has stepped into taking full responsibility for his own state of mind, no longer blaming Captain Picard for his seeming "loss." Healing is not linear. Healing is now!

"The Course says, "My Self is ruler of the universe. It is impossible that anything should come to me unbidden by myself. Even in this world, it is I who rule my destiny. What happens is what I desire. What does not occur is what I do not want to happen." W-253

That's empowering. My Self, my divine Self, is ruler of the universe. Even in this world, nothing is out of place. If I see a smile, I desired to see a smile. If I see a grin, I desired to see a grin. If it rains, I desired it to rain. If it is sunny, I desired it to be sunny. Everything is exactly as I have asked it to be in my mind. How can I be a victim if my Self is ruler of the universe, even in this world? That is beautiful. It covers all the bases. Everything comes to me as I have asked.

And now we will ask for happiness because we know that it is a real option *now*. It is not somewhere unreachable. We have a powerful mind, and we are going to use it to ask for what we truly want, which is peace! We deserve peace! It is our natural state of mind.

Chapter 9

FREQUENCY

Key Themes

- Miracle Working
- The Script is Written
- Opening to Real Communication

Movie Synopsis

It is 1999 and John Sullivan, a New York homicide detective, needs help. Recently separated from his girlfriend, Samantha, he feels that his life is falling apart. John, who still lives in the house he grew up in, discovers his father's old ham radio. A miracle occurs when his father, Frank, a New York fireman who seemed to die thirty years previously in a warehouse fire, suddenly speaks to him over the airwaves. For Frank it is 1969, which is the day prior to his death in the fire.

The two are at first incredulous, not believing that the other is who they say they are. However, as they continue to join over the radio it is clear they are receiving a rare gift of connection, as unbelievable as it seems. John tells Frank to take another route through the warehouse fire and his life is saved, due to the advice. As the two continue to join over the radio, events on the timeline continue to change rapidly. They work together across time to solve a serial murder case that impacts their lives in a personal way.

This movie culminates in a happy dream scene where the willingness to communicate has healed the ego's faulty perception of loss and pain, and Love is ever present as a shared experience.

David's Movie Commentary

If we can get a glimmer of what *Frequency* is teaching, we can save ourselves thousands of seeming lifetimes, because this movie is about the collapse of time.

No one told us when we were growing up that we would be miracle workers. Even now, the ego will say, "Who, me? A miracle worker?" But Jesus says that we can heal the sick and raise the dead, because we made sickness and death and can therefore abolish them. When we start to have miracles bursting into our consciousness, we can do things in ways we could never have imagined.

In this movie, the sick were healed and the dead were raised through the decision of two people to join together in a Purposeful and powerful way. That level of joining is available for all of us. That is why we are watching movies like this. Now is our time; this is the moment of great Awakening. Spirit is with us, beneath us, carrying us. No matter how deep the roots of fear go, they will be uprooted, pulled out, and released. Our whole life, whatever we envision for the rest of our life, will begin to open and expand in amazing ways. Never in a million years could we imagine what's coming next. It's the most glorious thing! Our life's Calling and Purpose are here!

The Holy Spirit is invisible, and cannot be perceived with the five senses, but when we start to give our life over to be used by Spirit, we know the Presence is there by all the miracles, effects, and reflections. The synchronicities start to get our attention, just like they got Frank and John's attention in the movie. Just turning our mind around—turning it right-side up from this upside-down guilt—is amazing when we give our life to it. Our life can take a totally different trajectory than we imagined.

Neither Frank nor John was expecting to join and heal. When they first told each other their names over the old ham radio, each of them had enormously defensive reactions. John, in disbelief, asked, "Is this some kind of joke?" and Frank said, "You're messing with me. You stay away from my son." That's how the ego reacts when we start to turn our mind over to Spirit. But as crazy as it felt to them at the beginning, it didn't take long for Frank and John to truly connect. But they quickly moved beyond that, which turned out to be a huge inroad into their mind, into their consciousness.

Love was right underneath the panic, and that is the way it is in our relationships that seem to be blocked. Once we start to open up, our communication may not sound articulate, or even make sense, but that is because when we first begin to expose our private thoughts, it doesn't necessarily feel good. We may think, "The Holy Spirit wouldn't say this and I can't believe it's coming out of my mouth, but this is what I feel." In order to heal, we must stop hiding and protecting. That's the first step.

What we discover is that where we expected rejection, we find a lifeline. Just when we think we will die, the Spirit says, "No, no, no." In *The Matrix*, when Neo is pulled out of the sinkhole and he's lying there, he asks, "Am I dead?" And Morpheus answers, "Far from it." That's how it feels when we start to really communicate in relationships. We ask, "Am I dead yet?" and Holy Spirit answers, "Far from it."

Communication has been so pushed down into the unconscious that when it hits the surface, when it comes into conscious awareness, it's intense. The ego is strongly tempted to shut it off. It says, "No. Don't start communicating now." But the Holy Spirit says, "Oh, yes. We are going to communicate and join and connect so well that the ego is going to dissolve in the face of that light and communication."

Communication is not limited except by belief. The physical aspects of communication, both verbal and nonverbal, are crude. As we go deeper on the spiritual journey, we start to realize what Jesus meant when he said, "All minds are joined." He meant that all communication is telepathic.

When we get into Purpose, it starts to dawn on us in an experiential sense that we are only ever communicating with our Self. "All that I give is given to myself." W-126 We've all probably had the experience of someone asking us for help and, although we want to be helpful, not knowing what to say or do. But then a profound wisdom starts pouring through, and the person soaks up every word. Suddenly, we realize, "That's the answer to *my* problem." What we have said to *them* is the very thing that *we* needed to hear. We have received the answer that we have been praying for. In the act of helping we discover that as we give, we receive. We experience that we *are* our brothers and sisters. We can't make personal survival our goal; there is a much greater plan. At one point in the movie, Frank was thinking of saving only his wife, who was a nurse, from danger. Johnny asked, "What about all the other nurses?" and then a miracle occurred and they too were saved.

This movie also takes a look at the idea of "the script is written." The script is the past and, the deeper we go into awakening, the more we start to realize that the whole point of forgiveness is to let go of the past. We have to let go of the belief that we can fix, change, or rearrange it, or spin it out in a different way. Those are only ego attempts to preserve the past and lock us into it.

The script to come—what we call the future—is also the past. That is the trick of time. There are those who seem to be clairvoyant and able to foresee the future. This is possible because they are not reading the future, they are reading the past. The ego put the present in between the past and the future to make it seem like they were different. One is already gone; one is yet to come. It's a pretty sneaky trick that makes us plan for the future with things like life and health insurance because we fear that the negative outcomes we've known in the past could come again in the future. This reinforces the fear and keeps the mind trapped in a linear construct of time that the ego invented!

This movie addresses the question of whether *any* meaningful choices can be made in form. That is, if we change our mind, does the script change or is it already written? As Frank and John attempt to join across decades, and experience more and more miracles, it seems as though they are actually changing the script. As we train our mind to accept the miracle, our perception becomes rearranged, it straightens out. It is no longer linear or fragmented or broken apart by the same old mistakes seeming to repeat over and over. It certainly seems like there are choices we make in form, but the plan is pre-arranged. As we go deeper into our mind, we become very in-tune and telepathic, and because we are watching the script, we can feel things coming before they seem to happen. We may still seem to be making decisions, but we are more detached from those decisions than ever. More and more we become the observer, the dreamer.

The movie shows multiple lives happening simultaneously. At first this seems strange, but the more we let our mind go with it, the more we notice how natural that communication feels. We are so used to thinking of time as linear; that what is over and done is fixed, almost like an old photograph. We see in this movie that father and son have great, miraculous connections over the radio, and everything seems to change. For example, at first John believes that his father died in a fire thirty years ago, and all the characters reflect that belief. After they begin communicating, Johnny tells Frank to take another route through the warehouse fire and his life is saved, due to the advice. That is just the beginning of the miracle scenes. John's perception is being turned around; the Holy Spirit is rearranging his perception. Now we are ready to put things into action, to resurrect the mind—no more depression, struggles, frustrations, doubts, difficulties, or concerns. We are right on the cusp of a great awakening, where we are starting to see our own power in terms of our mind and our consciousness.

The Course tells us that at this point, the teacher of God starts to see his escape, his whole way out. M-4.I.A.6 When we start to have that turn in consciousness—from feeling trapped and beaten down to seeing our whole way out of the dream that seems to have been going on for millennia—our joy radiates.

Jesus says that we touch people and circumstances we aren't even aware of. When our heart starts opening up, we start to feel lightness; we start to be washed of the guilt and heaviness of the past. More and more symbols of lightness, love, and joy come in, leading us to the experience of Oneness.

Through Frank and John's determination to join and to overcome obstacles, everyone arrives at the happy dream scene at the end of the movie. Their joining has made a complete connection that transcends time entirely. The script seems to reflect a very beautiful loving light, as well as a happy change in perception. At the beginning of the movie, the original family home was very dark, which was a reflection of Johnny's grief over the death of a life that could have been. He was missing a father that wasn't there. At the end of the movie, however, the house completely transforms into a house of light and love.

Chapter 10

ATONEMENT
IS THE ONLY CHOICE

The only question we should ever ask ourselves about anything is, "What is it for?" Goals that rely on an outcome in form will not make us happy. Happiness depends on keeping our Purpose of healing out front. It doesn't have anything to do with the world. Being in Purpose takes us right into the Atonement.

We finally reach a point where we give up all sense of future goals, of analyzing the past, of trying to change the world or making a better future. Those are all bad habits because they're egoic habits. They are all attempts to change what is simply the past. In the end, we can't change the past, we can only forgive it; we can only let it go.

This gets really deep. Our everyday life begins to seem more like a fairytale. It gets more and more surreal because our mind isn't focused on outcomes. In fact, we realize that we wouldn't even know what a good outcome is. What would that even mean? If all outcomes are the same, then why would we think that there could be better outcomes to pursue and worse outcomes to avoid? We surrender that belief. We let go of future goals concerned with productivity or making the world a better place. Instead, we choose to be in the moment and enjoy it to the fullest.

The Course speaks of the borderland where there still seems to be decisions to be made, but there is an awareness in mind that those decisions have *already* been made. Most of us have had the experience of watching things happen and thinking, *Of course*. That is because there is a part of our mind that has stepped back, like an observer. People show up on cue. We have a thought of them, we turn, and there they are. We have a thought that we need something, we turn, and it's put right in our hand. It happens quickly. That's when we're zooming into the Atonement, because the Atonement isn't about linear choices. It isn't on the timeline.

The purpose for which the world was made plays out as the script. When we see that all decisions are already made, it is very relaxing. We realize that any effort put into trying to improve anything is a complete waste of time. That is why Jesus says to accept the Atonement. I love that word: accept. Jesus says, "What could you not accept if you but knew that everything that happens, all events, past, present and to come are gently planned by One Whose only purpose is your good?" W-135 Jesus is zooming us in. He's saying the journey through time and space is almost over. What could we not accept if we but knew Who walks with us? "If you knew Who walks beside you on the way that you have chosen, fear would be impossible." T-18.III.3

So we're back to happiness. Spirit is saying, "Enjoy, enjoy, enjoy! Don't take it seriously. Don't take any of the seeming decisions in the world seriously. Accept, accept, accept." It's very restful. We can't mess it up. In the end, we come into complete acceptance and see that we never really made a mistake. There is no sin. This recognition is the acceptance of the Atonement.

Chapter 11

NEXT

Key Themes

- True Purpose
- Holy Relationship
- Collaboration

Movie Synopsis

Cris Johnson, a small-time magician in Las Vegas, can see into his future two minutes at a time, with one exception—he once had a vision of a particular woman walking into a diner at exactly 8:09. Knowing nothing other than this, he goes to the diner twice a day at 8:09 to wait for her. In the meantime, Cris puts his psychic powers to work by gambling in local casinos, where his two-minute advantage allows him to win against the house.

Callie Ferris is a focused FBI agent who, having discovered Cris' psychic ability, wants to enlist him in an effort to stop terrorists from detonating a nuclear weapon. Cris, however, is not interested in working with the authorities, having been studied and probed as a child due to his psychic abilities.

Liz Cooper is the woman from Cris' vision. When he finally runs into her at the diner, the encounter sets in motion a journey where Cris will learn how to trust and collaborate fully in new ways. With Liz, he can see further into the future than he's ever seen, and with Callie he experiences that service to the whole is the way to happiness. He sees that he has been squandering his mind in fear and avoidance and that joining in a higher purpose is the only thing that will "save the day!"

Introduction

This movie looks at psychic abilities, which are natural abilities symbolic of our mind opening toward a higher state. Parapsychology and psychic abilities, such as psychokinesis and telepathy, have been known and experimented with for a long time. Scientists say that we use only a tiny fraction of our brain; in metaphysical terms, we would say people are not using the full potential of their minds. The mind has enormous potential, and having a psychic ability is a sign that limited beliefs about what is possible have been released.

Consider this: You're going through your life, and then you meet somebody. There is something there, a feeling like, *We have something to do together.* It can be a feeling of deep connection. Cris feels that with Liz, but he doesn't know what the importance is. He doesn't know that she is going to link up with him in a relationship of trust that is going to be the key to his breaking out of his fear and paranoia about his psychic ability and the people who have probed him.

Cris and Callie, however, are going to be at odds because Cris perceives her as part of the government and the authority that he wants nothing to do with. This movie will show us that even those we perceive as our enemies are part of a greater plan of awakening, and that we share a purpose with them. Cris and Callie seem to be working against each other, but then we see how they move beyond that to a state of forgiveness; a place where they join in a higher goal that literally brings them together and takes away all animosity and struggle.

This movie is full of quantum physics, which gives us a new perspective on time. Likewise, the deepest teachings of *A Course in Miracles* are about the belief in linear time. Linear time is based on the belief that cause and effect are separate, that there is causation in the world, and that for every action there is a reaction. The world is based on this false cause-effect relationship. But underneath that is an experience of time being simultaneous; it's all happening at once. The ego tries to make time seem linear to lock us into the illusion. Each time we make the illusion real in our mind, we re-enact the separation, and we feel guilty.

The deepest teachings that have come through me have always been about hypothetical thinking, which is the imagining of different scenarios. Jesus talks about it in the "Clarification of Terms" section of the Course. He says that the Course is written *as if* there is individual consciousness. But there isn't; that belief is part of the trick. There is really only one mind, and it has fallen asleep. The ego has fragmented this one mind into what seems to be six billion minds. It's all part of this "as if" trick, as if the separation has occurred. That "as if" is addressed in this movie. It's spectacular.

David's Movie Commentary

Scene: Cris has been gambling in a Casino, where the surveillance team has been watching him. They believe he is cheating and pursue him. He uses his psychic ability of seeing two minutes into the future to evade the security men and escape to his house.

Because Cris knows where everybody is going to be, it's easy for him to get out of the casino. But let's look at his psychic ability. Jesus would ask, "What is it for?" Cris is using it as a trick to escape because he fears a negative consequence for himself. He also uses it to make money by placing small bets in local casinos. He doesn't go for the big jackpots because he doesn't want to get caught. It is almost as though he is toying with his psychic ability.

Psychic abilities may develop on the spiritual journey. However, the ego is sitting back in the mind looking for ways to take advantage of these abilities to see the future, to manipulate images, to manifest. The ego can have a heyday with that.

Let's look at Cris' motives. He doesn't have a higher calling at this point. He doesn't have a good use for his psychic ability. That's where Liz comes in. The Holy Spirit uses her to help Cris see that there is a much greater purpose for his psychic ability. The Holy Spirit doesn't frighten Cris by coming right out and saying, "We can use your psychic ability for enlightenment." Instead, Spirit introduces the idea in manageable steps that Cris can relate to.

Scene: From his house, Cris looks into the future and sees that FBI Agent Callie Ferris has discovered where he lives and is coming to ask for his help with the terrorist plot. He sees that he will be caught if he stays to speak with her, so he leaves before she arrives.

This two-minute window in which he was thinking, "I want to see why she is coming," is a good example of a hypothetical. Not only do we hear Callie play out all her thoughts in the hypothetical two minutes, but we also get to hear Cris play out his thoughts. We hear his distrust of the people who tested him. In effect, Cris is thinking, *Really, don't mess with me. I'm already feeling strange with this psychic ability. I don't feel loved. I don't want to have anything to do with your game, whatever it is. Even if, as you are claiming, it is to save lives.*

Our mind makes up two types of hypotheticals: In one, we are convinced that certain things actually happen. In the other, we just think about things, we fantasize. We let our mind run away, and cover over our spirit with our imagination. The sleeping mind *believes* in hypotheticals. It believes that what it sees around it is actually happening. The Holy Spirit has to show the mind that it is *all* hypotheticals, that none of it is actual. It is all "what ifs."

In human consciousness, "what ifs" seem to be going on in the mind, and there seems to be an actuality in front of that. In other words, we could say, "Well, I thought about reading this book." The reading seems like an actuality in this moment, a reality in one sense, and not a potential. It is not like, "I am potentially here reading this book" No, the mind is convinced, "I'm here, reading this book."

The deeper we get into it, the more we will see that the cosmos is a motion picture of what the mind believes, prefers, and selects. Perception is very selective. So of all the trillions and trillions of potential situations, the mind has locked onto one that it calls *actually happening*, but it is the same as the rest. It is just a potentiality based on preferences.

Once we loosen our mind from thoughts, beliefs, and preferences, we are selecting a miracle. There is actually a state of detachment in our mind that is the miracle we can select. But in order to select it consistently, we have to let go of the preferences, of all the preferred situations, such as hot or cold or sunny. All the preferences that are part of the ego hierarchy of illusions are distorting the perception and making some potentials seem like actualities.

In this movie we have already seen Cris act out some potentials. This is very much like a metaphysical meditation practice. He kept coming back to the same diner because he had a premonition of meeting Liz there and he felt that it was important for some reason, although he didn't know why. He was very devoutly practicing—not because he understood it but because he knew it was important.

This is a direct parallel to the spiritual journey. Even if we don't seem to see the fruits or the rewards, there is something inside us that knows it is very important. It's really beautiful how vigilant Cris was by coming back to that diner every day at the same time, hoping that she walked in the door so he could find out what it is.

Scene: Cris has finally met Liz in the diner. She offers him a ride to Flagstaff, saying she has some errands to run first, and it might take a few hours. They start to build a rapport; Liz begins to see something sweet and honest in Cris. Due to a severe storm, the road is blocked and they are forced to stay in a motel. Cris spends the night sleeping in the truck, giving Liz the motel room. The following morning they open to a deeper feeling of connection with each other. Lying in bed together Liz says to Cris, "Maybe there is such a thing as destiny." Cris opens his eyes and stares at the ceiling.

Remember this scene where they lay in bed with Cris looking up to the ceiling; we will see it again in the movie. It's a key setup regarding hypotheticals.

Cris and Liz have a budding relationship. Cris is trying to loosen things up a little by telling Zen jokes. The interaction between them is nice and gentle and easy. We see that they have just begun to follow the prompts of the Spirit, and we see that they have actually been brought together for a very high calling, for a very high purpose. Cris will discover that with Liz his psychic ability is powerfully enhanced.

The FBI wants to capture Cris to use this power. They have set up surveillance and surrounded the little motel room. We could see these things as Cris' doubt thoughts manifesting. We will see a lot of these doubt thoughts acted out. This is what the ego does. It tries to turn us against our brother, to turn us against our sister, to have us dismiss them. It wants us to experience fear and panic so we drop the relationship. There is a section in the Course called "The Healed Relationship," and it talks about what happens when the Holy Spirit is invited into a relationship. When two people shift the purpose of their relationship from special to holy, both partners are appalled. Fear leads the ego to say, "Get rid of your brother. Sabotage the relationship," instead of hanging in there for mind training.

In the movie the relationship is just starting to grow under the Holy Spirit's purpose. But there will be a major ego sabotage attempt to try and break the trust, to break off the relationship.

We're about to see a great example of how we have to just let the private thoughts arise. In this case, when the ego tries to sabotage things, Cris and Liz come back to link up to the deeper feelings they had, the feelings of love and connection.

Scene: *Later that morning, Liz goes out to get groceries and is intercepted by FBI agents who try to enlist her help in capturing Cris. They tell her he is a delusional sociopath and that everything he has told her is a lie. They give her a powerful drug and tell her to put it in his drink.*

Liz goes back to the motel and puts on a happy face for Cris, but she has underlying thoughts of fear and is just trying to go along with the instructions. Cris, however, is actually following the deeper guidance. He feels a deep connection with her. He waited so diligently to meet her because he knew they had a higher purpose.

In this scene, Cris is pretty tuned in, but Liz isn't. She is frightened. She has gone back to the motel room to do what she was told to do, as a lot of us would. We are conditioned to do what we are told to do. We believe things. We go through the motions. We have fear come up, but we think, "Well, I've got to survive and make it through," so we put on a mask, we put on an act. But we can see the fear in her eyes.

Jesus says, "Whoever is saner at the time the threat is perceived should remember how deep is his indebtedness to the other..." T-18.V.7 It's beautiful that Cris is so tuned in.

Scene: *Back at the motel, Cris and Liz kiss. Cris asks, "Is there something wrong?" Liz responds, "No. No. I'm fine."*

Spirit uses the kiss as a barometer of Liz's authenticity. This is the first time that Cris senses something is off. Notice how intuitive he is.

I want to highlight this moment. Liz has put the drug in Cris' juice. Terrorist sharpshooters are aiming at him. The FBI is surrounding the motel. It doesn't look good for Cris. But remember that the Holy Spirit has been invited into the relationship. Watch the power of the Holy Spirit. Liz is spouting a few more people-pleasing lines, but Cris is staying with sincerity and innocence. He is still in his purpose. And now comes the moment of trust. Who is Liz going to trust? She has evidence on both sides.

There are a lot of subtleties here. The Holy Spirit can see a much broader range of things. It's as if we have a complex equation or a complicated parable—and also someone to clarify the key points. The Holy Spirit can use anything, even an action adventure movie, to go diving down into the mind. It's quite miraculous.

A miracle is a state of detachment. It's like having a glimpse of being the dreamer of the dream, or the experience of a lucid dream in which we are aware that we are dreaming. That's what a miracle is. We could be anywhere, anytime, doing anything, when we have a moment—even a fleeting instant—of feeling that it's all a dream. That's a miracle. It's that calm state of watching. It's that sense of being aware that it is just a dream.

It seems that initially we just get a glimpse here and there. But then, as it says in the Course, miracles become habitual. We become habitually miracle-minded. It's great! We become absolutely joyful, carefree, and happy for no earthly reason. We can't wipe the smile off our face! And it has nothing to do with an outcome. It's so dreamlike and happy. That is what the miracle feels like.

The purpose of letting our unconscious thoughts and beliefs come up, not hiding them, is to clear away the debris in the mind. With practice we can maintain that state, regardless of what seems to be happening. It wouldn't matter if bullets were flying or if a nuclear device went off.

Scene: *Cris is about to drink the juice with the drug in it and Liz stops him. She opens her heart to him and tells him that the FBI has told her he is a sociopath, but that she doesn't want to believe that. She also tells him that the FBI will shoot him if he runs. Liz asks Cris if what the FBI has said is true. When he merely stares away, without answering her immediately, she feels that maybe she's been mistaken in her choice to trust him. As he begins to explain his ability, she thinks he is delusional. Even after he proves his ability to her, she still thinks it's a trick. He states clearly, "You know we don't have time for that. You said anything was possible." Cris gives Liz very specific instructions to follow once he leaves the motel. He tells her that if she can wait, whether it's a day, a week, or a month, he will find her. Then he leaves.*

Cris and Liz have joined in trust. Jesus says in the Course, "Patience is natural to those who trust. Sure of the ultimate interpretation of all things in time, no outcome already seen or yet to come can cause them fear." M-4.VIII In the miracle—and in this movie there is a collapse of time so we can see that ultimately there is no *already* or *yet to come*—we are in the moment. That is where we are invulnerable. That's where our strength is. That's where we are as God created us, as Spirit, as Mind.

So when there is pain involved, it is in the mind; it means that we've chosen the ego's lens. Pain is never of any value. We can go through an experience and say, "That was painful, but it served me well," but pain never serves us well. We decide the lens we are going to look through. When we go through the initial phases of mind training, where we let all the darkness that was pushed out of awareness rise up, the ego interprets it as horrific. It tells us that the pain, thoughts, beliefs, and memories are real. But it's just a clearing process. Jesus says that pain is unnecessary, although the process is usually experienced that way.

It's extremely rare to think of releasing the ego without some vacillation, some back and forth. Jesus is realistic. He is telling us that doubt thoughts are always a false perception and not to throw in the towel when the process seems to be painful. Our mind has been upside down for millennia and now it's just beginning to turn right side up. Having our whole perception turned one hundred and eighty degrees is a huge shift. As that turn is going on, the ego interprets it as painful. And as long as we're identified with the ego, we feel its pain.

It's not even *our* pain, because we are the Christ. We don't have any pain. But as long as we are misidentified with the ego, we feel its emotions. For example, if we notice ourselves saying, "I am angry," we have to recognize that it's not true. It would be more accurate to say, "I am mistakenly identified with anger." Likewise, to say, "I'm in pain," is false identification. It is not even honest. Jesus says in the Manual for Teachers that honesty means consistency. That means that everything we think, say, do, perceive, and feel is all in alignment. That is what honesty is.

Being consistent starts to break us out of the mold of, "Do you honestly want to know how I feel? Well, I'm in pain." Or, "I am honestly angry at you." Jesus says that is not possible; we're never honestly angry. We're just tricking ourselves if we think we are angry and that we have a good, justified reason to be so. He says in the Course that anger is never justified. We have to believe that certain conditions are in effect before we can even get angry, including the belief that there is something outside of us that has hurt us, which is just a belief.

Nostradamus, a sixteenth-century Frenchman with the gift of prophecy, didn't just predict what was going to happen the next week or the next month. He predicted things centuries ahead of time, before they were even invented. He described airplanes, missiles shooting through the sky. He tried to describe these things in words centuries ago. Well, it was a psychic ability, and I don't think he was peaceful. He was quite disturbed by these things. He was tapping into the lode of fear.

In the movie, Cris can see two minutes into the future, and with Liz there, he can see further into the future, and yet it brings him to the humble state of asking what the purpose is. What is the purpose for the psychic ability? What is the purpose for any of this? That is what the Holy Spirit is working with us on: to use all the skills and abilities that the ego made, including time, to *undo* the ego. The ego made up time and the Holy Spirit knows how to work with that.

The metaphor of "the script is written" leads us into a new perspective. We start to open to the witness self, the watcher, because we realize that if things are destined, we can't change the script. We start watching our thoughts and being attentive, and by doing so we start to change our mind about our mind. That is where the full focus and effort needs to be. The value of "the script is written" is that it shows that everything we perceive is the past. Everything is the past, and our only responsibility is to release the past. Isn't that fun?

If we follow the Course diligently, soon we will become unambitious. Extremely unambitious. We talk about being ambitious, fighting, striving, struggling, achieving, accumulating, and winning. Jesus says, "No." He says, "I need do nothing." T-18.VII "Simply do this: be still." W-189.7 This is a mystic's mind saying, "Aren't you glad to know that the ego mind made all this up? Aren't you glad to know that you *can't* change it? You can only change the way you look at it." It's glorious! Think of all the stress and pressure involved in trying to make the world a better place, in trying to make our life better, in trying to improve ourselves.

Who is the self that needs to improve? Is it the Christ? Does the Christ need self-improvement classes? Does the Spirit need to go to workshops and seminars over and over? No. That's the ego. Needing to make a better self is an ego thought: *Am I skilled enough, rich enough, smart enough, worthy enough?* It is a trick to keep the mind distracted from the stillness. The Bible states, "Be still and know that I Am God." Psalm 46:10 It is that simple.

The miracle collapses time and rearranges perception, and ultimately this leads to the realization that it is all the past. Once we have that awareness, our mind sinks into stillness. We won't be trying to fix or change the past, rearrange it, or make a better configuration. We flow into an experience of enlightenment and Self-realization, and it's beautiful! It is the witness Self, which watches with no sense of trying to make it different.

One of the most profound lines in the Course is, "Seek not to change the world, but choose to change your mind about the world." T-21.in.1 That was profound for me. I had spent a lot of time protesting and having opinions, telling people, "No, you've got it wrong; we have to save the whales." Save, save, save! But the Course says that the *mind* needs salvation. The world is a distractive device, tempting us to put all our energy into trying to make changes where change is impossible.

Instead, we must tune into guidance. Inner listening is where our decision-making gets simplified. Everything that could conceivably come in time and space is already given. That's pretty simple. That's why we don't give in to the temptation to try to analyze it in form.

Following the Holy Spirit is a path of surrender and yielding, away from resistant thinking, away from thinking, *I'll do it my way*. We have to keep opening and surrendering. That is the dismantling of the ego. The ego will be fighting and kicking and screaming all the way because it wants to be in charge, but the Spirit is saying, "No, loosen."

It's never about what will happen in the future. It's about letting go of the belief that we can control time and space. The whole point is to listen and follow, and to be taken to a state of mind, not to a particular outcome. The Holy Spirit sees that all outcomes are the same in form. There is no difference. But in terms of state of mind, there is a big difference between love and fear, and between the purpose of the Holy Spirit and the purpose of the ego. It is a major difference, and that is what Guidance is aimed at: teaching us discernment, teaching the difference between the right mind and wrong mind, between love and fear.

Guidance helps us to stay happy, to stay in the flow. Sometimes there seems to be no end to the ego attempts to disrupt the Holy Spirit's guidance. But those are just thoughts. They have no power to dictate anything to us. We have to see them for what they are and not buy into them, not buy into any fear. That's our purpose! If we just listen and follow, we glide along, and it is so easy. When the mind gets into fear and takes that fear seriously, the world will reflect those fearful thoughts. That's why we want to let them go.

There has to be the willingness to not buy into the world, to not feel like we have to change the world or make it a better place. We need to pay attention to our mind and pay attention to our intuitive feelings; we need to start using them as our barometer, our gauge. That is tuning into guidance. Our feelings are a great barometer as to whether we are tuned into the Spirit or not. So we practice with that. More and more, we can start to let go of outcomes.

When we are happy, the whole world is happy. Isn't that great metaphysics? And wouldn't God be cruel if we could be smiling and happy, and others could be in misery and pain? Who set that up? That doesn't sound like a very good God. That doesn't make any sense. If love is real and love is all that there is, then that is great. It's about opening to that experience.

Then we can let go of all sense of pain, suffering, victimization, or abuse; we start to realize that is the past. Who wouldn't be happy to let go of that? Since when does pain, suffering, and abuse feel good? It doesn't. We need to let it go. And that is the whole message. We need to give ourselves permission to let go of any thought, any perception, that isn't extreme happiness. It's not worth it to give our holy mind over to such foolishness, to such egoic thoughts and beliefs.

The underlying metaphysics are that it is all made up, and we have to take one-hundred-percent responsibility for our state of mind. Lesson 136 says that sickness is a defense against the truth. In that lesson Jesus describes the whole dynamic, about how defenses are like little magic wands that we wave. The mind makes up a whole scenario, symptoms and whatever, and forgets it. Jesus even uses the term "quick forgetting." Then the ego projects the cause out onto something in the world. It's as if the pain, discomfort, or symptom had to come from something in the world.

We must purify our thoughts. Purify our mind. Purify our consciousness. This is a practical teaching, because it is all a state of mind. Everything we think, believe, feel, and perceive is all connected, based on what is going on within. In the end we will have the experience that there is no within and without. We will no longer see the world as "out there." We will start to realize that ideas leave not their source and the world is in our mind where it has always been. Then the world is benign. Then the world is a friendly world. If we have a friendly mind and the world is in our mind, then we have a friendly world. It's just common divine logic.

That's why we have *A Course in Miracles*. It's a mind training tool to take us inward to that state of mind. And it works! That's the good news! And we rejoice together. We laugh together. We play together. It's all just props. When we go to the theater, it's just props that are on the stage; they aren't real things. These props can be used in a relaxing way as a backdrop for mind training. They are for mind training. They are given as part of the plan. They don't come through struggle or trying to make things happen. That is a nice way to live our life. "Ah, it is given. Thank you." Can it be that simple? Yes! That is the way it goes when we surrender. It's fun, too. It is meant to be fun!

He had been using his ability only for himself, but when she joins with him, he opens up to the purpose of serving the greater good. When we join in purpose with our brother, we join with the Holy Spirit, and we will experience miracles that will collapse time. Jesus tells us in the Manual for Teachers that we cannot even choose the form of the curriculum, which is a reason to relax; everything is already pre-arranged. All we can do is be willing to open up and go with the plan. And if we fight against it, it's too late. We have already invited the Holy Spirit in, and resistance is futile.

Cris was holding on to his grievance about being tested, probed, and abused by others. Because of this belief, he was afraid to say yes to something that would bless beyond himself. If we think that everyone else is different from ourselves, then we won't understand shared purpose. Everything we do with the Holy Spirit is for everyone. Every miracle we share blesses the whole universe.

The Holy Spirit is using all of the scripts, all of our willingness, to take us to that state of wholeness where nothing can be added or taken away. This is what higher purpose is about. The FBI is going to close in because Callie wants to use Cris in a collaborative way to prevent a nuclear explosion. This is a higher purpose, but it still has elements of protectiveness. She wants to protect the people of Southern California. And she has been coercive. She has told him that if he doesn't do it she'll throw him in jail.

The Holy Spirit's plan is for us to come to a state of perfect peace and innocence; a state that has no ego components in it. Even though we don't know our own best interests, the Holy Spirit does. In every conceivable situation there is a purpose in our mind that is the answer. And this answer is beyond all hypotheticals. In fact, this answer, this purpose, shows us that all hypotheticals are the same. But this is a very high learning in mind.

What we *can* relate to is guidance. So if we seem to be facing a difficult choice between two options, the Holy Spirit will give us the most helpful option, until we finally realize that all the options are the same, that there is no choice between illusions.

Scene: Cris leaves the motel, and jumps off a cliff on the side of the mountain. He has asked Liz to send her vehicle over the cliff after he jumps, which in turn knocks down a water tower, taking an old wagon, a train caboose, and many large logs with it. Cris uses his psychic ability to dodge the items hurtling down the cliff. When he reaches the bottom, Callie is waiting for him. She is about to be crushed under the falling debris. Callie asks Cris to save her, and he does. He is then captured by Callie and taken to FBI headquarters.

The Holy Spirit never commands and never demands. Both characters are still reflecting an inner fear that is dictating their actions. They are both trying to be helpful based on what they believe is helpful. And yet, only the Holy Spirit knows what true helpfulness is—and that is to let go of all of the scenarios, recognizing that they are all the same.

Scene: Cris is hooked up to machinery at FBI Headquarters against his will, and is forced to watch newsreels on the television in order to locate information on the terrorists and the nuclear bomb. Using his ability to see into the future, he sees that the terrorists have captured Liz. She is on a rooftop parking lot, strapped to a wheelchair, with a bomb around her chest. He watches her blow up.

When Cris sees his girlfriend being blown up, instead of joining with Callie and sharing what he knows, he says, "You have to get me out of here!" He wants to handle it all by himself; he doesn't want the FBI using his psychic abilities. The agent is still afraid that eight million people will die. We're going to see these two play a cat-and-mouse game of who has the better abilities to stop the terrorists.

Scene: Cris escapes from the FBI building, with the agents in hot pursuit. He goes to the rooftop where he had the vision of Liz being killed. Callie arrives on the roof and Cris tells her about his vision of Liz. Callie tells him that it hasn't happened yet, and talks him into working with her.

Now we see symbols of collaboration; we see the beginning of the holy relationship between Cris and Callie. After they have gone through all this fear, they come to a point where they see that it's better to collaborate. This happens with all human relationships. We may be able to tolerate pain and suffering, but this is not without limits. No matter who we have a grievance with, it's better to let go of the grievance now and to collaborate with them, instead of trying to act against them, or in spite of them.

As Cris is reading the future, he is also reading the past. This is why *A Course in Miracles* teaches us that the script is written. All the scenes and scenarios of this world have already happened, including wherever we seem to be right now. This is just a scene from the past. But we're viewing it now as if it is happening right now. The ego divides the past up into the past-past and the future-past, and the now-past. We're watching the now-past right now.

The Holy Spirit uses the past, so that we learn how to join and collaborate. He takes us into a deeper, higher, purpose in which we see that it's all the past, before it disappears. But we have to learn that we cannot choose between different scenarios. As a person, we think we chose to be where we are now, and we may even have plans for later. It's all part of the trick. It's the ego with all its different hypothetical scenarios.

What will happen in the future has already happened. All we can do is forgive it, and see it with the Holy Spirit. Then the world will disappear, and we'll return to Heaven, and we'll be so happy. Heaven is our natural home. This world of hypotheticals is not our home. We have never found lasting happiness in this world.

Nor will we reach Heaven by dying. Some people think they will go to Heaven when they die. But Heaven is not reached through death. It is reached through forgiveness, through resurrection of the mind. Now we see why *A Course in Miracles* is so important. We will never escape from this world through the ego. The ego would have us forever reincarnating into this world, never finding God's Love. However, when we learn to decide with the Holy Spirit and collaborate, we will find the escape through forgiveness.

Now we see Cris and Callie collaborating. This is intuitive collaboration. Even Callie believes in his ability. She tells all of her agents to just follow him, to forget all the intelligence information that they have gathered, to forget everything and follow him. This is what we must do with the Holy Spirit: let go of all of our past learning and learn to follow *only* the guidance of the Holy Spirit, never being tricked by the ego. That's how we wake up.

Scene: *With precision, Cris uses his psychic ability to guide the FBI forces against the terrorists. In his mind, he splits himself off in all directions, searching for Liz in the abandoned warehouse.*

Cris says, "You search this floor, I'll do the rest," because he's going to search the rest with his mind. He's going to check out all the potential places where they might have Liz by using the power of his mind. The FBI agents can hardly believe it because they think it would take a whole team to do what he is going to do with his mind.

This movie is an analogy showing us the acceleration that takes place in spiritual awakening. The Holy Spirit keeps narrowing down our potential options for illusions, and helps us zoom into the correction in a very quick way. Each miracle that we experience with the Holy Spirit saves thousands of years in human terms. This is why it is important to tune in to the Holy Spirit. He will lead us to the inevitable correction, back into the Kingdom of Heaven.

The scene showing Cris in many places at once is about superposition. Superposition just means that there are all kinds of options. What we seem to see before our eyes is the selection of options that we believe is possible, based on what we prefer to happen. The world is not outside the mind. The only reason we can seem to read a book, from inside a body, from behind eyeballs, is because we believe that it's possible. But the Holy Spirit will show us that it is *not* possible. This is just one scenario out of the whole quantum field, and we believe that we are in it. We are not.

Scene: Liz has been rescued and the terrorists have been killed. When Cris and the FBI discover that the nuclear bomb has been moved, Callie leads Cris to a tracking device that is designed to help them locate the bomb. As Cris stares at the monitor, he says, "Something's wrong. I made a mistake. It's happening. Now." The bomb explodes, everything is torn to pieces, and the screen goes black. We see Cris back in the motel room. He opens his eyes and gazes up at the ceiling.

Here we are back at this crucial scene. Here is the key to healing! The whole last half of the movie was a hypothetical! If you were reacting at all to any parts of the last half of the movie, you were reacting to a hypothetical scenario. And now we see that Cris has been brought back to a point where he has another choice—another choice to collaborate, another choice to join, another choice to lay aside fear and to listen only to the Holy Spirit. So that whole scenario had no reality or existence, and that's what this whole world is: hypothetical scenarios that are playing out based on fear. No human being has a real lifetime; it's all hypotheticals in the mind. And the goal is to learn to forgive all of it, without exception. So now we will see where he goes from this moment. Will Cris choose to collaborate with the FBI?

Scene: In the motel room, with Liz lying beside him, Cris gets up and calls Callie, saying he will cooperate with her willingly. He tells Liz there is something he has to do. He says "I can't put it off anymore. It may be a week or a month. If you can wait, I'll find you." Cris goes outside and Callie arrives to pick him up. "You ready?" asks Callie. "Yeah," says Cris. They get into the car together, and the movie ends.

This is a deep movie. It really gets to our assumptions about time and relationships. From this movie we can see that instead of planning our future based on our past, based on our desires, based on preferences, based on the kind of life we think we want in the future, there is another way. The Holy Spirit is saying, "Are you ready? Are you ready for a new journey that is different from your past? Are you ready now to help in the plan of awakening, to let all your skills and abilities and resources be used for one purpose: the resurrection of the mind, coming to know yourself as you truly are, as God created you?" This movie is an example of how, when we resist the call to join, fearful hypotheticals play out. They are all empty roads; they don't lead anywhere.

At the end of these roads, we simply seem to die and start another scenario. And the scenarios go on and on, until we decide that we are ready to wake up to forgiveness. The world is not escaped through death. Sometimes people commit suicide, thinking they are going to find a way out. That attempt won't work. We just come back with another scenario and another nightmare, because all the scenarios are based on fear. That's why we have to come back and do the scenario again.

The nuclear explosion in Los Angeles was just another fearful scenario, another hypothetical. When we learn to follow the Holy Spirit, we will have a happy dream. This is happening now. When we learn to forgive completely, there will be so much joy that we will think we can hardly stay on earth, hardly stay in the body. We will see that we cannot be guilty for these scenarios, because the ego made them all up, and we are not the ego. We are Spirit. And this world has never been our home. We can dream a different world if we allow the Holy Spirit to be the purpose of our dreaming.

Chapter 12

I AM RESPONSIBLE
FOR THE WAY I SEE

Quantum physicists say that the quantum field is all energy, where everything is absolutely unified. The Course talks about it as the forgiven world. Quantum physics shows us that the old way of thinking in terms of people, situations, and places does not serve. We can't think in linear terms. We can't think apart from Truth and be happy, because we *are* the quantum field. Everything is absolutely connected. Still presence is just still presence. It's not associated with persons, places, or things. It is what it is. We cannot prepare for it without putting it in the future. To bring the Holy Instant into our awareness, we just have to desire it. Then we come into this deep, wonderful still presence that is not circumstance-dependent. It doesn't matter whether the body seems to be in a castle, a school, or a convent; in Europe, Japan, or America. It's not circumstance-dependent because all these things are just hypotheticals.

Hypotheticals are essentially questions, and all questions are of the ego; there are no questions in the quantum field. All questions come from the belief that we could be apart from the Whole. In our natural state of mind, there are no questions. There's nothing to fix, prepare, change, or avoid. We can just rest in contentment. Now. What a happy realization that there *is* no Europe, Japan, or America!

Only the mind that is out of touch with the quantum field—and deceived into thinking that there are actually people, places, and situations—can feel guilt. There's some kind of responsibility associated with that. The Course says, "I am responsible for what I see. I choose the feelings I experience, and I decide upon the goal I would achieve. And everything that seems to happen to me I ask for, and receive as I have asked." T-21.II.2 Some misinterpret the first sentence, "I am responsible for what I see," as meaning that we are responsible for the starving children, the wars, and all the destruction in the history of the universe. But we are not responsible for the world. We are not responsible for the error, which is false, fragmented perception.

The correct way to interpret the sentence is that we are responsible for *the way that we see the world*. We are responsible for accepting the correction, for seeing the world with the Holy Spirit. That's the only thing we can be responsible for. What about the starving children? No. What about the issue of the scientists versus the believers? No. What about our family? No, not responsible for our family. What about our house? Nope, not responsible for our house. What about the health of our body? Nope. We are only responsible for seeing the world the way the Holy Spirit sees the world. That's the only responsibility that we can ever fully accept. Every time we try to take responsibility for something other than that, we have misplaced our responsibility; we have chosen guilt. Staying aligned with the Spirit, staying tuned in, is really what it's about.

Chapter 13

X-MEN: DAYS OF FUTURE PAST

Key Themes

- Healing Ancient Hatred
- Letting Go of Control

Movie Synopsis

The X-Men are mutants, a subspecies of humans who are born with superhuman abilities, who fight for peace and equality between regular humans and mutants in a world where anti-mutant bigotry is fierce and widespread. They are led by Professor Charles Xavier, a powerful mutant telepath who can control and read minds. Charles' archenemy is Erik Lehnsherr (Magneto), a powerful mutant with the ability to generate and control magnetic fields. Charles and Erik have opposing philosophies regarding the relationship between mutants and humans. While Charles works towards peace and understanding between mutants and humans, Erik views humans as a threat and believes in taking an aggressive approach against them, although he has found himself working alongside the X-Men from time to time.

In the year 1973, Sentinels—robots that were created for the purpose of killing mutants—are released. The Sentinel program was originally conceived by Dr. Boliver Trask, who in the early seventies was one of the leading weapons designers. He had begun covertly experimenting on mutants, using their gifts to fuel his own research. There was one mutant who discovered what he was doing. This mutant had the ability to transform herself into anyone she wanted. Her name was Raven. She hunted Trask across the world, and at the Paris Peace Accords in 1973, she found him and killed him. However, killing Trask did not have the outcome she expected; it only persuaded the United States government of the need for Trask's program. They captured Raven, and then tortured her and experimented on her. In her DNA, they discovered the secrets to her powers of transformation, which gave them the key they needed to create Sentinels that could adapt to any mutant power. Over the next fifty years, the Sentinels killed multitudes of mutants, as well as humans who tried to protect them. But it all started that day in 1973, when Raven killed Trask. That was also the day she became known as Mystique.

One of the X-Men, Logan (Wolverine), is sent back to the year 1973. His specific task is to find and establish harmony between Charles and Erik, who are arch-enemies at that time. Their cooperation is crucial in preventing the mutant Raven (Mystique) from killing Dr. Trask, which will set up a domino effect resulting in decades of war.

Saving the world is seemingly the mission of Logan, Charles, and Erik. Their real mission, however, is the deeper inner work of letting go of control and coming into an experience of True Forgiveness.

Introduction

This movie illustrates a spiritual journey that involves going back in time. The Purpose of the journey is to find the core grievance and let it be healed. When the grievance is healed in Forgiveness, all future scenarios of conflict and destruction are also healed. It is not that they have been prevented in time; it is that we have come to the realization that there was no time in which they could have existed. In the Happy Dream, everything is resolved. It becomes harmonious and then disappears.

Wolverine is the agent strong enough to go back through time and ignite the mission of forgiveness. We can think of ourselves this way as well. We can imagine that our future self, or our higher Self, is orchestrating this whole thing for our awakening. We are just perceiving it in time, where we perceive ourselves to be. There is great love and compassion coming from the higher Self, the future self.

The mutants start with a great premise: End this war before it ever begins. We can adjust the words to say: End this *world* before it ever begins. Jesus awoke and said, "Before Abraham was, I Am." T-3.III.6 This is what *A Course in Miracles* is about: Ending this world before it ever begins. Going back to the *I Am-ness* before the world was.

We have been tricked into believing that the present moment is in between the past and the future. When we went to history class, the teacher drew a timeline and the dot in the middle was now, in between the past and the future. But what if the past and the future are the same? And what if now is not wedged in between them? What if we have been tricked about the present moment? What if the present moment is before time was?

We read *The Power of Now* and struggled to be in the now, but maybe the now is not where we thought it was. Maybe it is somewhere completely different. This is deep! What if we can end the war by seeing it never began? What if we can end the world and the cosmos by seeing that they never existed? What if we could recognize that we are actually an eternal creation and that we have never been bound by time or space or form? We have had amnesia. We have forgotten the *I Am-ness*, which is all that is and all that will be. We got caught up in what seems to be a world in which there is a power that controls us.

This movie is saying we have to go so deep that we transcend time and space; we have to Forgive the belief that they could ever have happened. This Forgiveness renders even the thought of a core grievance impossible. Innocence remains as the only Reality and we see that control was never an option.

David's Movie Commentary

Scene: Raven, appearing in the form of a colonel, violently frees a dozen mutants who are being held captive by the army. She puts them on an escape plane but does not join them, saying, "My war is not over, the enemy is still out there."

This line, "My war is not over, the enemy is still out there" is significant. As long as we take sides, as long as we believe there is conflict in the world of form between the mutants and the humans, or this country versus that country, this culture versus that culture, this person versus that person, we do not know where the war is. There are no wars in this world. The only war is a war against our Self, which is due to our belief in the ego. We use the symbols of this world to prove that we are not our Christ Self, and we are determined to succeed.

Workbook Lesson 139 says, "You are yourself. There is no doubt of this. And yet you doubt it." The whole linear cosmos of time and space is about self-doubt; it is about not knowing who we are. It is about trying to make up another self, other than the one God created, and trying to be damn sure that we succeed in being little and small. In fact the mind that is sleeping and trying to dream a different world apart from Heaven wants to be right so much that we seem to keep shifting from one dream to the next. We can call them incarnations.

Each incarnation is an attempt to prove that we are right about our small identity. Every second of every day is, *No, no, no* to God. That is all the tick, tick, tick, on the clocks are: *No, no, no, I am not whole, I am not complete, I am not eternal, I am not Christ, I am not perfect. No, no, no.* And the *yes* would be the accepting the Truth: *I am as You created me; I am Spirit. I cannot be right about my identity in this world because it does not exist, has no reality, and never will have a reality.*

As long as we see people as being outside ourselves, we are still going to experience conflict. We blame the other person, but the murderer is not on the battleground in form. The murderer is the belief in the ego, which is the sponsor of the belief in separation, the whole time-space pseudo identity, the whole dream. When we believe that the ego is true, we believe that there is no God. We cannot hold onto both; there cannot be eternal love and ego.

When we believe in the ego we believe in a death wish. It is self-deception on a magnitude we cannot even imagine. Forgetting we are the Christ and thinking we are a human being is an error of huge magnitude. It is not real, but as long as we believe in it, we will remain in a self-induced sleep and experience self-inflicted drama. This movie demonstrates the need to find the murderer within, the controller within, the mis-creator within. We need to look inside for the answers, which means we must go inside and discover our real power that was given to us by God.

This murderer within, this false identity, has to be exposed. So every time we seem to get angry at a brother or sister in this world, Spirit asks us to look again, reminding us that we never hate our brother for his sins, only for our own. It always comes back to that mis-identification. All the anger, hatred, and rage arise from us choosing to be small.

Scene: Wolverine's consciousness has been sent back to 1973, to the younger version of himself. When he arrives at the Xavier mansion to speak to Charles, Hank (Beast), a mutant who lives with Charles does not want to let him in. Wolverine punches Hank, telling him, "You and I are going to be good friends in the future; you just don't know it yet." When Charles appears, he tells Wolverine to get out. Wolverine explains that he's been sent by the future Charles. To convince Charles that what he is saying is true, Wolverine tells him intimate details of his life that Charles has never told anybody. Wolverine says he needs Charles' help to find Raven and that they will need Erik's help also. Charles initially refuses, but eventually agrees so that he can help Raven. He still believes Erik is an evil man who cannot be changed. Wolverine tells Charles that he and Erik sent him back to the past together. Erik is housed in the basement of the Pentagon under arrest and they enlist a fellow mutant, Swift to help free him.

It is daunting to be sent back in time on a mission to facilitate the healing of a relationship between two arch-enemies. In Wolverine's case, it seems like an almost impossible task due to the intense hatred between Charles and Erik, but he is very focused on his Purpose. He is aware of a higher plan and is there to hold the high note.

Charles and Erik have been called together on a mission of forgiveness in order to save the world. There may be so much anger and animosity between arch-enemies that finding forgiveness may seem impossible. However, our enemies are actually our saviors; they are there to help us heal our perception of the world. To see *it as* unified, we need to see our Self as unified. That is the bigger plan, no matter how personal it feels or how much hatred and animosity there seems to be.

Even though it is not our initial experience, we know at some deep level that our enemies are us. They are actually our dear friends. In the future, we will all be laughing together at past scenarios and marvelling at what a joy it is to be together, feeling such deep love and connection.

That is what the human race is about now. We are really one Self, but we are acting as though we are not. We are acting as though each one is different, apart, with all kinds of judgments. It is all a pretend game. The Christ in our mind is saying, *You can wake up. You can stop this charade any instant you want. It is not a matter of time; you just have to want to stop it.*

This desire to wake up is what draws us to look in our mind and ask, *Is there anybody in my life right now that I really do not want to see or talk to?* Those people we are avoiding are actually there for our awakening!

We are sent from our higher Self, in our present conditions, to discover love. There is great love underneath all the hatred. "The holiest of all the spots on earth is where an ancient hatred has become a present love." T-26.IX.6

This movie is about perceiving destruction and conflict and realizing that we have to go much deeper to find the solution. It is not going to be a "good guys beat the bad guys" solution. It is going to be about moving inward in consciousness, beyond the projection of time and space, to wherever there has been a breach or a grievance in the mind. Jesus tells us, "You will look upon that which you feel within." W-189.5 If we have hatred, we will see a world of hatred; if we have love, we will see a world of love. We have to go to the core.

Jesus also tells us that "... it is so crucial that you look upon your hatred and realize its full extent." T-13.III.1 We do not need to be frightened when our hatred starts to come up, when we shake and tremble, when we feel we would be crushed if anybody knew our awful feelings. We must allow our feelings to come up so that we can move through them. We will find mighty companions around us, and we have the strength of the Holy Spirit and God within us. It is inevitable that we will transcend our hatred. That is why we can't back down.

That is what the mutants, even Wolverine, have to learn right away. When Wolverine went from a dismal future back into an antagonistic situation, we heard the Roberta Flack song, "The First Time Ever I Saw Your Face" play. This was a reminder for Wolverine of coming back to Innocence and Truth, to the Christ vision that is beyond appearances.

This movie is a big tweak in the mind. Instead of trying to look for the solutions in form, on the surface of consciousness, we realize: *I am going to have to go much deeper. I am going to have to actually go before time was to find the solution.*

Scene: *Wolverine, Charles, Beast and Swift go to Washington, DC, where Erik is being held in a high security prison deep beneath the Pentagon. Swift uses his mutant powers in ways that appear to rearrange time and space in order to facilitate a masterful prison break for Erik.*

In *A Course in Miracles* Jesus says that if you allow yourself to perform miracles, he will arrange time and space for you. You may wonder what arranging time and space might look like. Hollywood gives us an example on the big screen, as Swift becomes a miracle worker, saving the day by diverting the bullets from their targets.

Scene: *Wolverine, Charles, Beast and Erik board a private airplane to Paris in an attempt to stop Raven from killing Trask. Shortly after board-ing, Charles and Erik begin to allow all of their feelings of mutual hatred and abandonment with each other to come to the surface. As they do, it seems as if the structural integrity of the plane is being compromised and everything becomes unstable.*

An underlying deep hatred and feelings of abandonment come up in Charles and Magneto. Even though they are friends in the future, they now are arch-enemies who despise each other. Both have had a relationship with the same woman, Raven, and they both have misperceptions. Conflict is a misperception of who we are, projected out onto characters in the world. It seems as though we are battling each other when really the mind is at war against itself; believing in the ego, believing in time and space, and projecting the conflict onto interpersonal relationships.

We have never actually had an interpersonal conflict with anyone, ever. The belief that we have is a big trick to keep us asleep and dreaming, to keep us projecting our self-hatred for having made up a self apart from God and trying to exist apart from Heaven. That is a lot of hatred. We project it out onto characters and think we have enemies. These enemies can seem to take the form of authority figures, family members, or anyone who we have a grievance with. But they are only reflections of the hatred in our mind being projected out, as we see in this scene. Now that they are in the same proximity, Charles and Erik are letting some of their rage come to the surface. Earlier, Charles said, "I hate violence," but when the elevator doors opened and he saw Erik, he punched him, as if he was totally unaware of his rage.

Scene: *Charles and Erik calm down after they've said their piece to each other. The plane restores itself and Erik invites Charles to play a game of chess with him. They begin to have honest communication with each other about how their lives have been over the past ten years. They appear to be in agreement that they need to stop Raven before she kills Trask. Erik apologizes to Charles for everything that has happened between them.*

The hatred being projected between them is now starting to soften because they are both sensing they were misperceiving each other and that there is something bigger and more important, going on. This is pointing to the bigger picture. Our purpose is even deeper than changing history; our purpose is to go back *prior* to history. To wake up from the dream, we have to get back to the *I Am-ness* that is before time was. But in this initial phase, Charles and Erik are open to stop projecting their hatred onto each other.

Raven is fighting for the mutants to try and protect them. She is trying to kill Trask because she believes that will be helpful to the mutants. The projection of self-hatred is what all wars are about, even though they seem to be about something else—protecting a country, overthrowing a dictator, defending against Hitler, Mussolini, Osama bin Laden, and so forth. One time Gandhi was asked if there was such a thing as the devil, and he replied that if there is a devil, he is running around in our own hearts. There is not an external devil.

We have to see that the murderer—the ego—is within, and it is projecting the whole cosmos out. As long as we keep taking the bait and keep the ego hidden from awareness, then we think our "enemies" are external. And we think certain enemies have to be brought down. That is what Raven is thinking. She is a representation of the belief that there is an external enemy that has to be destroyed.

Now Charles and Erik are beginning to put aside their ancient hatred. They are realizing that they need to collaborate and join on a much deeper level to bring an end to the future war. They are starting to understand the whole context of the projected war. They see that the only way forward is to forgive from the heart, let go of control, and release the idea that there is an external enemy.

This movie shows us very clearly what our task is: to forgive ourselves for believing we could separate from God and make up a world of complete unreality, one that has no resemblance to Heaven whatsoever. We have to forgive that whole belief, which means we have to go back to the "I Am-ness" before time was. That is the only way to heal it.

We know the story of Jesus and Judas, the apostle. When anger arose in Judas, Jesus did not perceive it as real; he could not be betrayed because he did not believe in betrayal. As he said in the Course, "The message of the crucifixion is perfectly clear: Teach only love, for that is what you are." T-6.I.13 There was no betrayal, no victimization, not even any pain. From a healed perception, he could see the situation as a whole and be in that *I Am-ness* that we are talking about that is prior to time, that is pure divine Love and innocence.

We see the betrayal theme enacted in many movies, including *Brother Sun, Sister Moon,* which is about the Franciscan community. Paulo lived in Assisi and was opposed to St. Francis and his group all along until, in a dramatic moment, he said to the Pope's guards, "I am with them." The scene beautifully conveyed his realization that he was one with his brothers. There is no betraying, no turning bad, or going evil. These are just opportunities to forgive the murderer within, the death wish within. The trap is trying to find the good guys or the bad guys and taking sides.

Scene: Wolverine, Charles, Hank and Erik find Raven about to attack Dr. Trask during the Paris Peace Accords. As a struggle ensues, a traumatic memory is triggered in Wolverine that renders him completely useless to the mission in the moment. Erik who had been collaborating, sponta-neously makes up his own plan, believing the only way to stop Raven is to kill her. Hank knocks the gun from Erik's hand. The gun fires and Erik who has the power to control metal, directs the bullet down and out of the window that Raven has jumped from. The bullet hits her in the leg. Erik pursues Raven with the intention to kill her. Chaos breaks out in the street where crowds of people were gathered for the Peace Accords. Hank attempts to stop Erik from killing Raven, down amongst the crowds.

Here we see Wolverine slipping into memories of being mistreated and tortured. These memories can be justifications for rage. When anger arises, we can lose all awareness of forgiveness. Even if we have had a strong spiritual practice for many years, it can all go out the window when we are raging. We have someone in front of us and we say, "How dare you! How dare you!" We can forget our practice, no matter how many years of mind training with Jesus, Buddha, Krishna, or Ramana Maharshi we have.

This is what is happening to Wolverine: He is losing sight of the context of his mission even though he is the one who was sent to bring the context of forgiveness. His assignment was to go back in time and correct the original error.

While Wolverine is out of Purpose, Erik, who has a lot of pride and arrogance, begins to follow his own plan; he has also lost sight of his Purpose. As long as we are joined in Purpose, in integrity, the plan flows. But when we discard the plan and try to do it our way, things go awry. There are examples of this throughout history. Someone says, *I've got a better plan. I've got a better way. I don't need the group to tell me what to do,* and then tries to enact it for the whole group. Going our own way, rather than following Spirit's plan, allows the ego to slip in again and sabotage everything.

It is not that external wars break out or that global economic crises occur. All these are just perceptions, just interpretations, to draw us away from the awareness that we have a mission to heal, to be the savior of the world. Our mind has the power to heal and save the world if it just sees the false as false. It takes only one teacher of God to save the world, and we are it. Not us personally, but the mind, which is powerful.

Scene: *Charles attempts to calm Wolverine. When Wolverine comes out of his flashback, he initially has no idea where he is or who is with him. Suddenly his mind is restored and the purpose of his mission returns.*

I've heard people say that we have to spread *A Course in Miracles*; we have to get it into the hands of the Pope. No, we have to get it into our own heart. It is our own hatred, our own attack thoughts that we have to go in and find. And when we release them, the whole world, the whole distorted perception, is released. How many teachers of God does it take to heal the world? One. Just one who is willing to see the world anew with the Holy Spirit.

People ask, "But if Jesus did it already, why are we still here?" We are not still here. It is over. Salvation has been accomplished. We need only to accept the happy joyful truth that it is over and that we do not have to fight for it. It has been done! The distorted perception has been neutralized. In fact, it is so neutralized it never was. The "I Am-ness" was never touched, never deceived, never harmed. It is still pristine, as it always was and always will be

Scene: *Charles wants to take another dose of the drug that allows him the use of his legs. However, the drug blocks his powers, which allow him to join his mind with the minds of others. Wolverine asks him not to take the drug because his powers are critical in locating Raven.*

So this is the decision we must make. Are we going to do it for the whole? Are we going to regain the power of our mind, the power to forgive? Are we going to go for the great awakening or are we going to continue to choose for personal betterment, personal comforts, personal achievements? Are we going to continue to hold onto the mask, to make the mask better, to strive to be a better person? Self-improvement does not solve anything. The Self that God created does not need to be improved; it is already perfect. It is pointless to focus on bettering ourselves in any way.

In every decision we make, we are either choosing for the whole or choosing to retain a personal self. We have to choose for the whole. Charles is coming out of his depression in this scene. He was trying to keep the use of his legs to retain his personal identity, but he decided instead to choose for the whole. Now he is in his wheelchair seeking to regain the very strong power he has of being able to search and locate minds. His gift is the ability to transcend private thoughts.

Scene: *Raven is at the airport on her way to Washington, D.C., to kill Trask. Charles has regained his powers. Wolverine and Hank are by his side as he hooks himself to an apparatus that allows him to speak to Raven through the bodies and voices of different people at the airport. He tries to remind her of her goodness. He tells her that the girl he grew up with was good, fair, full of compassion, and would never kill. He says she needs to come home.*

This is a beautiful scene where Charles is reaching out to Raven. Sometimes on this pathway people say to me, "I wish I could hear the Holy Spirit in my mind. I wish I had a direct connection to the Holy Spirit"—as if they need to have a personal connection to the higher Self.

We are not necessarily going to hear the Holy Spirit's Voice inside our head. This scene reminds us that the Holy Spirit can come through our brothers and sisters, with guidance and direction—we can trust it! The Holy Spirit is all around and can reach us in many ways. In this scene, Charles is reaching out to Raven in an amazing way in an attempt to help her change her mind about going after an external enemy.

Scene: When Charles appears before her at the airport, he implores her not to kill Trask. He tells her that killing Trask will set her on a path from which there is no return, and create an endless cycle of killing until there is nothing left. He says they can stop it right now, together. Raven ignores him, saying that he hasn't changed at all and that she knows what she needs to do.

The movie is bringing us into a deeper lesson. Wolverine and Hank are saying, "Shut her down, shut her down," and Charles wants to do it but he doesn't think he can. He says, "I am too weak." Charles has taken a step in the right direction by embracing his powers, however, there's still a desire in his mind to control Raven. Whenever we believe we can change a person, change the world, even make the world a better place, we still do not get it. We are still playing at control; we are still playing God—the small version of God—controlling the images, believing we can control or shut people down.

This is no different than sending out hit men to shut somebody down. It is no different than trying to shut down a nuclear reactor or a military program. It is the use of force and control. That is where Erik is going; he wants to have control over the Sentinels; that is his version of safety for the mutants. He is still going for the weapons path. And Raven is still thinking, *I know what I have to do.* She still wants to murder Trask.

A strong desire for control is being exposed here. Raven still plans to kill Trask, Wolverine and Hank are trying to get Charles to shut Raven down, Charles *wants* to shut Raven down, and Erik wants to control the Sentinels. *It is the wish for control that needs to be undone;* it is the group's ultimate mission. This is what they truly came together for—to release and forgive the need for control in the mind. The old pattern of control, of thinking we can change somebody or the world, is all coming to an end in this movie.

Scene: The President of the United States is at a ceremony in Washington to unveil the Sentinels that Trask has created for the government. Charles, Wolverine and Hank are in the crowd. Charles is scanning the crowd, searching for Raven's mind. When he finds her masquerading as a secret service agent, he controls her by freezing her body so that she cannot shoot Trask. Meanwhile, Erik has raised an entire sporting stadium into the air and is directing it towards the ceremony. Erik is controlling the Sentinels also, and they begin shooting at the crowd. In the ensuing chaos Charles loses his mind control of Raven and she continues her pursuit of Trask. Erik drops the sporting stadium around the ceremonial events, sending rubble and metal flying everywhere.

Charles is enacting the control mechanism one more time. This has been acted out throughout time: Attack, defense, attack, defense. A strong attack calls for a bigger defense. It is all part of the same system. But what is the best defense? No defense! That is the meaning of "In my defenselessness my safety lies." W-153 That is what meekness is. Remember that two thousand years ago Jesus said, "The meek shall inherit the earth." T-2.II.7 He means that they will literally overcome history and linear time with their strength, with their *I Am-ness.*

So we can guess where this movie is heading. It is not going to be one of those typical good-guys-win, bad-guys-lose movies. The transcendent power is going to come through the voluntary relinquishment of control, attack, and defense, and making the choice for meekness.

Erik has really lost it at this point. He has been fighting to protect the mutants, but now he is attacking the mutants. How easy it is to be misguided with power and control. There is no true loyalty, no true consistency, no integrity; there is nothing. The ego is a mad puff of an idea that is a death wish. What do you expect of a death wish?

There are books in which spiritual teachers tell us to love our ego. How are we going to love it? It is a death wish! We have to dispel it. We have to pull our mind away from it; we cannot love it. We have to literally forgive it, to see past it and give it no reality, no belief. It is healed only through defenselessness.

Scene: *Charles is pinned down under the rubble of the sporting stadium. Erik has pierced Wolverine with metal scraps and thrown him into the nearby river where he is drowning. Raven, who is disguised as the President, shoots at Erik, hitting him in the neck and he falls to the ground. The Sentinels shut down as he is knocked out.*

124

When Raven points her gun at Trask, who is standing amongst the govern-ment officials, Charles projects his image in front of Trask and pleads, "Raven, please do not make us the enemy today. You have saved the lives of these men. You can show them a better path. I've been trying to control you ever since the day we met, and look where that's got us. Everything that happens now is in your hands. I have faith in you, Raven." His image falls away, leaving Raven eye-to-eye with Trask. She is deeply touched by Charles' words, pauses, and voluntarily drops the gun. At the instant of that decision, all of the future attack disappears.

Once the desire for control was seen and released, a ripple effect went out from the new decision in the mind. Raven dropped the gun voluntarily. The world has been saved. Mission complete. The murderer within has been uncovered and stopped.

This scene beautifully demonstrates that when we drop attack, we drop the ego—and all its effects disappear. The mutant's future of destruction disappears. All of it disappears with the decision to forgive. We have to forgive all belief in guilt and attack, and come to this place in our mind of stillness, of completion, of innocence. When we do, the world we perceive will change. We will never again perceive abuse, conflict, war, or neglect. All the false effects of the ego vanish when we see the impossibility of the ego.

The whole point of the mission was to prevent the attack, but Charles finally realized he couldn't control the outcome. He said to Raven, "I have faith in you." And that is what Jesus is telling us, "I have faith in you. You will make the same decision that I made, to remember Heaven and go back to God." Time and all the effects of time will be gone when we make that decision. This is a great illustration of the core lesson in life, which is to forgive. It ends the future!

This is Quantum Forgiveness. It can undo all of history. It can undo Adam and Eve. It can undo Hitler. It can undo anything in our seeming personal history where we feel we were mistreated. It can undo everything! What an adventure!

Chapter 14

CONCLUSION

Awakening of the Mind may seem as if it is just trickling along slowly and tediously, but there is an availability for an exponential shift. The spiritual journey can be much, much faster than we imagine. I started on the path to awakening in the mid 1980's and kept at it with great determination. But now, people who reflect a celestial speed-up are coming into my awareness. There is no longer a sense that waking up has to be a long and difficult journey. There is an energy, a momentum, that can be felt. It is like a wave of joy washing over us—it's tangible.

The journey can be fun! I use many tools that are enjoyable and engaging. One of them is the *Movie Watcher's Guide to Enlightenment*, which is a booklet that Spirit gave me as a pathway back to God. There is an online *Movie Watcher's Guide to Enlightenment* as well. (mwge.org). When you feel a negative emotion come up and you are tempted to panic, shut down, or push it out of awareness, you can go to the online Movie Watcher's Guide instead. You can use the index to look up the emotion you are feeling, and it will refer you to specific movies that will help you move through that emotion. This online resource is unique and quite sophisticated.

Many years ago, I was guided by Spirit to develop two worksheets. To experience a permanent state of peace and joy, we must be willing to let go of what we think we know. The *Instrument for Peace* and *Levels of Mind* are two profound tools for tracing a present upset back to a belief in mind so that a conscious decision can be made to release it.

Even a tiny upset can feel like a giant sliver in the mind. The *Instrument for Peace* is a tweezer for the mind: it has the uncanny ability to isolate and pluck an upset from our mind and then to expose the concepts or core beliefs underneath. Core beliefs can be hard to get at precisely because they are so heavily defended by the ego. The ego is acutely aware that once we pull the plug on all our unquestioned beliefs, the game is over. That's why it has built a heavily defended fortress of fear around the core beliefs that make up our self-concepts.

Levels of Mind takes us inward from what we perceive is happening on the screen all the way back to the desire that something be different than it is right now. Once we see that we are desiring something other than peace of mind, we can choose again.

The happiness of Quantum Forgiveness is available and accessible now. No longer do the thoughts of time call for our attention. Presence has come into awareness at last. Relax and enjoy a supremely miraculous experience—Being Totally Present.

I am with you all the way on this remarkable adventure!

Love and Blessings,
David

ALSO BY DAVID HOFFMEISTER

The Answer
Going Deeper
Only One Mind
Healing in Mind
A Glimpse of Grace
My Meaning in Scripture
Purpose Is the Only Choice
Unwind Your Mind Back to God
Awakening through *A Course in Miracles*
Movie Watcher's Guide to Enlightenment

David's writings are available in print, e-book and audiobook formats. Select materials have been translated into Chinese, Danish, Dutch, Finnish, French, Hungarian, Japanese, Norwegian, Portuguese, Spanish, and Swedish.

ONLINE MATERIALS

acim.me
acim.biz
mwge.org
livingmiracles.org
miracleshome.org
awakening-mind.org
acim-online-video.net
davidhoffmeister.com
a-course-in-miracles.org
store.livingmiraclescenter.org

MOVIE ACKNOWLEDGEMENTS

Solaris (2002)
Twentieth Century Fox | Lightstorm Entertainment
Writers: Stanislaw Lem (Novel), Steven Soderbergh (Screenplay)

Source Code (2011)
Vendome Pictures | Mark Gordon Company
Writer: Ben Ripley

Mr. Nobody (2009)
Pan Européenne Production
Writer: Jaco Van Dormael

Frequency (2000)
New Line Cinema
Writer: Toby Emmerich

X-Men: Days of Future Past (2014)
Twentieth Century Fox
Writers: Simon Kinberg (Screenplay & Story) Jane Goldman (Story)
Matthew Vaughn (Story)

Next (2007)
Paramount Pictures | Revolution Studios | Initial Entertainment |
Virtual Studios
Writers: Gary Goldman (Screenplay) Jonathan Hensley (Screenplay)
Paul Bernbaum (Screenplay) Phillip K. Dick (Novel)

Star Trek: Deep Space Nine: Season 1, Episode 1: "Emissary" (1993)
Paramount Television
Gene Roddenberry (based upon "Star Trek" created by)
Rick Berman (Creator & Story)
Michael Piller (Creator, Story & Teleplay)